12 Questions

New Christians Frequently Ask

12 Questions

New Christians Frequently Ask

by Sylvia Bambola

Heritage Publishing House

For information contact:

Heritage Publishing House
heritagepubhouse@gmail.com

Sylvia Bambola
sylviabambola45@gmail.com

ISBN-13: 978-0-9657389-1-0
ISBN-10: 0-9657389-1-4

Also by Sylvia Bambola

Non Fiction:

Following the Blood Trail from Genesis to Revelation

Fiction:

Mercy at Midnight
The Babel Conspiracy
The Daughters of Jim Farrell
The Salt Covenants
Rebekah's Treasure
Return to Appleton
Waters of Marah
Tears in a Bottle
Refiner's Fire

To

My children and grandchildren,
with love

Table of Contents

Introduction

A person is spiritually saved and becomes new after understanding he cannot save himself, then asking Jesus to come into his life. He has come to accept, by faith, the five immutable tenets of Christianity: 1) Jesus is the Son of God. 2) He came to earth as a man, born of a virgin, and was and is true God and true man. 3) He died on the cross for our sins and is the only way to heaven. 4) He rose from the dead. 5) He ascended into heaven but will come again.

It's a wonderful moment for the new believer. Sometimes, it's accompanied by a "spiritual" feeling, such as an overwhelming sense of God's love. Sometimes it brings on a bout of weeping and a deep sense of gratitude. And sometimes the new believer feels as though nothing has happened or changed. That's because God is not a cookie-cutter God. Jesus makes His presence felt in different ways. But know for sure this momentous occasion is indeed momentous and recorded in God's *Book of Life*. There is even a celebration in heaven as the angels rejoice. The new believer is now part of the family of God and can look forward to an eternity in heaven.

But after the excitement dies down, the believer is told he must now stand on the Word and walk out his faith. A bit confusing. How can one stand and walk at the same time? And what does God's Word say, exactly? That's when all the questions begin.

Oh, there are so many. I remember those early days and how often my mind felt like it had been microwaved. Since then, I've come to understand that a lifetime isn't long enough to fully learn and understand God's Word. The deeper I dig, the more I realize how little I know, though it makes for an exciting journey.

But for a new believer, the journey can be confusing. That's why I wrote ***12 Questions New Christians Frequently Ask.*** It's a place to start. A place to find a few answers under one cover; answers to such questions as, "How can I increase my faith." "How do I pray?" "Is Satan real?" And more.

Though much can be added in answer to each of these questions, my purpose was to give the reader just a basic understanding and pique his interest in searching the scriptures more deeply on his own. It's basically a springboard designed to launch the new believer into the Bible and discover the wonders of God's Word, it's power and truth and incredible ability to heal, restore and change lives.

May the journey be a happy and rewarding one!

Question One: *Is the Bible really the Word of God?*

"People say you can't trust the Bible because it was written by so many different people. Besides, aren't most of the stories just allegories, intended as an illustration or lesson?"

Make no mistake, the Bible is the infallible Word of God. You can trust it. Though it's comprised of sixty-six books and penned by forty different authors, it has incredible integrity. Even the Dead Sea Scrolls attest to this. They show the great care scribes took when copying the Scriptures because the wording hasn't changed but has remained intact from generation to generation. The Isaiah Scroll, discovered in Qumran, Cave 1, is the same book of Isaiah found in the King James translation, except for a few words.

But that's not the only proof of the Bible's inerrancy. Literally, hundreds of Old Testament prophecies have come true. One such example concerns the nation of Israel. Hosea 3:4-5, Ezekiel 37:11-12, and Ezekiel 11:17-20 predict the regathering of the Jews into their homeland. This has happened. In 1948, despite all odds, Israel became a nation, just as the Bible predicted over twenty-five hundred years before.

But the Bible contains many other prophecies, some regarding Adam, Abraham, Sarah, Noah, Moses, just to name a few. There are even three-hundred prophecies concerning Jesus' first coming, all of which have been fulfilled.

Any mathematician will tell you this is mathematically impossible. Stephen M. Bauer, in his book, *The Math of Christ*, examines just forty prophecies concerning Christ's first coming and concludes that, "the combined probability of all these forty events happening is one times ten to the 136th power. That's a 1 with 136 zeros behind it." He further clarifies it by saying, "all the atoms in our entire observable universe is a number considerably smaller than the odds of these forty prophecies coming to pass." In other words, it's absolutely impossible, at least in the natural. But we know that with God, all things are possible!

For an additional in-depth look at hundreds of fulfilled prophecies from Genesis to Revelation, check out Ken Johnson's book, *Ancient Prophecies*

Revealed. It should convince anyone of the inerrancy and accuracy of Scripture.

Okay, but are the people and stories real or just object lessons?

Jesus said they were. He spoke of Abel, Moses, Elijah, Jonah, Noah, Lot, Abraham, Isaac. Jacob, Zacharias, Daniel, David, Solomon, and the Queen of Sheba. And He spoke of them as real people. In addition, He mentioned places such as Gomorrah Sodom, Capernaum, Bethsaida, Chorazin, Tyre, Sidon, and Nineveh; some of which have been excavated by archeologists. And lastly, Jesus claimed that all the law and prophets spoke about Him, which covers another big section of the Bible. Jesus also spoke to Satan and cast out a horde of demons; indicating that they are also real.

In addition, Jesus quoted the Old Testament. When He was in the wilderness for forty-days and was tempted by Satan, He said, *"It is written, Man shall not live by bread alone, but by **every** word that proceedeth out of the mouth of God"* (Matthew 4:4). Here, in Matthew, Jesus was quoting Deuteronomy 8:3b, *"man doth not live by bread only, but by **every** word that proceedeth out of the mouth of the LORD doth man live."*

Notice that both Scriptures indicate that we are to live by **every** Word of God. In Hebrew it's *kolw* and means "all, every." In Greek, that word is *pas*, and means, "all, every." I think it's safe to say that every Word of God means **every** Word of God.

Jesus further confirmed this when He said in Matthew 24:35, *"Heaven and earth shall pass away, but my words shall not pass away."* He confirmed it again in John 14:24 where He said that His words were not His own but His Father's words. And yet again in Matthew 22:29 when He said, *"Ye do err, not knowing the scriptures nor the power of God."*

It really comes down to: *do we believe Jesus or not?* When He spoke about these people, places and demons, He believed they were real. And when He quoted Scripture, He indicated they were God-breathed. And quite frankly, that's good enough for me.

And finally:

The Bible changes lives. It certainly changed mine. I've lived on both sides of the street; one without Jesus and His Word, and one with. I can tell you there is no comparison. Though my lifestyle was not as dramatic or destructive as some, I can say that life without Jesus and His Word is often shallow, unfulfilling, and unsettling. On the other hand, knowing Jesus, which also means knowing His Word because He **IS** the Word made flesh, gives you an anchor, a hope and a wonderful future. But don't take my word for it. Ask anyone who has come to the Lord; who has been delivered from a destructive lifestyle. They will be happy to give you an earful.

Here are some things God's Word can accomplish:

It reveals our spiritual condition before we come to Christ. I Corinthians 6:9-11 describes this condition. It mentions fornicators, idolaters, adulterers, thieves, drunkards, etcetera, and ends by saying, *"And such were some of you."* And then our new condition, *"but ye are washed, but ye are sanctified, but ye are justified in the name of the Lord Jesus, and by the Spirit of our God."* Wow! Praise God for His mercy! There's not one person who has ever lived, other than Jesus, who has not committed sin, who has not fallen short of God's standards. Even so, there is no one who has fallen so low that God cannot change him. How wonderful to know that God has a remedy and we don't have to stay in our sinful condition!

It strengthens us and helps us grow. 1 Peter 2:2, *"As newborn babes, desire the sincere milk of the word, that* *ye may grow thereby."* And John 6:27 says, *"Labour not for the meat which perisheth, but for that meat* (spiritual food) *which endureth unto everlasting life, which the Son of man shall give unto you: for him hath God the Father sealed."* Who doesn't want to grow and mature and be all we can be? But like trees, sometimes we get twisted or bent along the way. Life has a way of doing that. But that's not what God wants for us. And He is able to unbend those twisted branches and help us grow into strong men and women of God.

It can heal us. Psalms 107:20 says, *"He* (God) *sent his word, and healed them, and delivered them from their destructions."* And then Proverbs 4:20-22 says, *"My son, attend to my words* (the laws and commandments of God) *incline thine ear unto my sayings. Let them not depart from thine eyes; keep them in the midst of thine heart. For they are life unto those that find them, and health to all their flesh."* Many people have a hard time believing that God truly wants them healthy and whole, but He does. Learning and studying God's Word can help us gradually come into this knowledge and faith.

It enlightens us and gives us joy. Psalms 119:130 says, *"The entrance of thy* (God's) *words giveth light; it giveth understanding unto the simple."* It also gives us wisdom, understanding and knowledge (Proverbs

2:1-6). Who won't want these things? Think of the traps and snares we could avoid by walking in the wisdom, understanding and knowledge of God! And Jeremiah 15:16 says, *"Thy words were found and I did eat them; and thy word was unto me the joy and rejoicing of mine heart."* Yes, God's Word can bring joy to our hearts!

It gives us victory over sin. Psalms 119:11 says, *"Thy* (God's) *word have I hid in mine heart, that I might not sin against thee."* And Colossians 3:10 says, *"put on the new man, which is renewed in knowledge* (by God's word) *after the image of him that created him."* Worldly wisdom can be confusing, contradictory and lead to destruction. It's only God's Word that keeps us anchored and our path straight because His Word changes not. We know where He stands. We don't have to guess. And if we stay planted firmly in His Word, we will have victory over sin.

It cleanses and sanctifies us. John 17:17, *"Sanctify them through thy truth: thy word is truth."* And 2 Peter 1:3-4 expands this. *"According as his* (God's) *divine power hath given unto us all things that pertain unto life and godliness, through the knowledge of him that hath called us to glory and virtue: Whereby are given unto us exceeding great and precious promises: that by these ye might be partakers of the divine nature, having escaped the corruption that is in the world through lust."* Oh, how many are the promises of God! And He is faithful. He will bring them to pass in our lives if we stay true to Him and His Word.

Other Scriptures to consider:

First, the Old Testament:

Psalm 33:6, *"By the word of the LORD were the heavens made; and all the host of them by the breath of his mouth."* God's word is a creative force. Think about the power it can have on our lives!

Isaiah 40:8 tells us that, *"The grass withereth, the flower fadeth; but the word of our God shall stand **forever**."* Remember, Jesus spoke about Isaiah as though he was a real person, and this is what God told him. Our life is brief, and the world constantly changes, but God's Word never changes, never becomes obsolete. It will be around for all eternity because forever is forever. And we can take comfort in that!

Psalm 119:89, *"forever, O LORD, thy word is settled in heaven."* Again, God's Word will be valid forever. It never changes. And all heaven can testify to it.

Psalm 138:2b, *"thou hast magnified thy word above all thy name."* Don't miss this. God puts even more store in His Word than He puts in His name, and that's saying a mouthful.

Psalm 33:4 says, *"For the word of the LORD is right; and all his works are done in truth."* That word "right" in Hebrew is *yashar* and means, "prosperous, just, pleasant, good," just some of the characteristics of God's Word, and what it accomplishes.

Psalm 119:105, *"They word is a lamp unto my feet, and a light unto my path."* God's Word is the lamp that shines light on our feet to guide us and keep us from falling. If we don't want to stumble from one problem to another, we need to follow God's Word. It lights our path so we can see where we're going, and not have to feel our way in the dark.

And oh, how encouraging Isaiah 55:11 is! *"So shall my* (God's) *word be that goeth forth out of my mouth: it shall not return unto me void, but it shall accomplish that which I please, and it shall prosper in the thing whereto I sent it."* Wow! God's Word is so powerful. If we let it, it will accomplish just what God wants it to in our life. It can bring health, deliverance, protection, direction, strength, guidance, and so much more.

It's the wise man who follows Psalm 119:11, *"Thy word have I hid in my heart, that I might not sin against thee."*

Now, the New Testament:

As previously mentioned, in Matthew 24:35 Jesus said, *"Heaven and earth shall pass away, but my words shall not pass away."* Jesus is referring to His Words in the New Testament. He's telling us that His Word is going to last even after the old heaven and earth are replaced by the new heaven and earth. He's saying His Word is enduring and inspired. We need to take it seriously. He also said in John 5:39, *"Search the scriptures; for in them ye think ye have eternal life; and they are they which testify of me."* What did He mean? He's saying that the Old Testament speaks about Him! In fact, the entire Bible, both Old and New Testament, is about Jesus! Again, He is validating the true and sacred nature of the Scriptures.

1 Peter 1:25 tells us that, *"the word of the Lord endureth forever."* It's a repeat, saying there's no expiration date. God's Word is permanent. He means what He says and says what He means. If God puts this much store in His Word, so should we.

Then II Timothy 3:16 tells us that, *"All scripture is given by inspiration of God, and is profitable for doctrine, for reproof, for correction, for instruction in righteousness."* If we want to live a righteous life, we need to know the Word of God. It will correct us, instruct us and give us a firm foundation.

Hebrews 4:12, *"For the word of God is quick, and powerful, and sharper than any two-edged sword, piercing even to the dividing asunder of soul and spirit, and of the joints and marrow, and is a discerner of the thoughts and intents of the heart."* Again, we learn that God's Word is powerful. It's like a sword because it can cut away our old thinking and habits. And it can reveal what's in our heart. And that's important because the Bible tells us that our heart is deceitful and wicked and only God really knows it (Jeremiah 17:9).

II Timothy 2:15, *"Study to shew thyself approved unto God, a workman that needeth not to be ashamed, rightly dividing the word of truth."* If we don't know God's Word, we will end up being ashamed. Why? Because we will be susceptible to every wind of doctrine (Ephesians 4:14) or even the doctrine of demons (I Timothy 4:1). We will be easily deceived and unable to stand when the going gets tough. And, sooner or later, the going always gets tough.

Conclusion:

So . . . is the Word of God true? Yes. The Dead Sea Scrolls validate it, Jesus validates it, the Word even validates itself through fulfilled prophecies. It has the power to radically change lives. It provides a guide out of our darkness and a firm foundation on which to live our lives. And it is powerful and full of promises for those who believe.

Question Two: *Do I need to be baptized?*

"I was baptized as an infant. Do I need to be baptized again after I receive Jesus as Savior?"

First, some background:

Baptism, or using the *mikveh,* has been defined as immersion in water to purify one from ritual uncleanness. Its roots are found in Leviticus, about 1400 years before Christ, and details what is ritually clean, unclean, the methods of ritual purification, and most importantly, blood atonement for sin via the sacrifice of animals. In this context, baptism usually involved total emersion.

The *mikveh* was used in the following occasions:

- After a woman had a baby
- By priests in relation to Temple rituals
- As spiritual purification before the Sabbath and other holy days
- For brides and converts to Judaism
- By anyone who came in contact with a dead body

But never was it used as a means of forgiving sins. Jews understood that it was only through a blood sacrifice, as laid down by Moses, that sin was forgiven. During the second Temple period, from the time of the Maccabees, around 150 B.C., to the destruction of the Temple in 70 A.D., the use of a *mikveh* reached its zenith. In fact, archeologists were astonished to find so many *mikvehs* in the ruins of 70 A.D. Jerusalem. Thus, we see that during the time of Christ, baptism, or the use of a *mikveh,* was widely practiced. It's ironic, because during this same period the priesthood was extremely corrupt.

Baptism in the New Testament but before Jesus' resurrection:

The word "baptism" mentioned in Matthew 3:11, Mark 1:4, and John 1:26 is the Greek word *baptismos* and means "to fully cover, to make fully wet, to wash, dip, used regarding ceremonial washing." This is the baptism which Jesus experienced in the Jordan. What Jesus was doing was ritually cleansing Himself for His ministry, which began soon after His forty days in the wilderness.

There is a big difference between John's baptisms and baptisms after Jesus' resurrection. In Matthew 3:11, John told the Pharisees and Sadducees, *"I indeed baptize you with water unto repentance, but he that cometh after me is mightier than I, whose shoes I am not worthy to bear: he shall baptize you with the Holy Ghost and with fire."*

John, of course, was talking about Jesus and the future infilling of the Holy Spirit. But unpacking this scripture gives us further insight. First, that word "water" is *hudor* in Greek and means **"rain, shower, rainy."** This was not the baptism of the Holy Spirit, but it alludes to it; giving us a foreshadowing of things to come. Both Joel 2:23 and James 5:7 talk about the Holy Spirit being poured out on all flesh in a former **rain** and latter **rain**.

Next, John was baptizing unto "repentance." In Greek that word is *metanoia* and means "reversal of a decision." John was performing the traditional baptism of that day and basically saying, "change your decision not to follow God to a decision to follow Him." John was not baptizing as a means of forgiving sins. That would have been unthinkable for him and those he baptized.

Interestingly, when Jesus came to be baptized, John didn't want to do it. In response, Jesus said, *"Suffer it to be so now for thus it becometh us to fulfil all righteousness."* (Matthew 3:15)

Here, righteousness is *dikaiosune* in Greek and means, "equity (fairness, impartial) in character or act; just; right." Jesus, in becoming immersed in water, in the *mikveh* of the Jordan, was telling John that even though this was unnecessary, He wanted to follow the law and do what was perceived as right, fair, impartial by ritually cleansing himself before beginning His ministry.

He was thirty, the age when men who were destined to become priests, finally entered the priesthood. Before such entrance, a purification ceremony in the *mikveh* was necessary. Jesus was already a priest after the order of Melchizedek (Hebrews 5:6-10). Did He really need a ritual cleansing into the priesthood? Of course not. But He wanted to fulfil the law in every detail. Hebrews 2:17 tells us that, *"Wherefore in all things it behoved him* (Jesus) *to be made like unto his brethren, that he might be a merciful and faithful high priest in things pertaining to God, to make reconciliation for the sins of the people."*

Jesus humbled Himself and did what every other man had to do in order to fulfill the requirements of the Aaronic priesthood as well as fulfilling every other detail of the law.

And then there's this: Matthew 5:17-18, *"Think not that I am come to destroy the law, or the prophets: I am not come to destroy, but to fulfil. For verily I say unto you, Till heaven and earth pass, one jot or one tittle shall in no wise pass from the law, till all be fulfilled."* Again, Jesus did everything right and never took a shortcut. He was careful to fulfil every part, every detail of the law, including the ones in Leviticus pertaining to ritual cleansing.

Baptism after Jesus' resurrection:

After Jesus rose from the dead, He instructed His disciples to stay in Jerusalem, and gave this reason, *"For John truly baptized with water; but ye shall be baptized with the Holy Ghost not many days hence."* (Acts 1:5)

When that day came, suddenly there was a *"rushing mighty wind,"* tongues of fire and the wonderful infilling of the Holy Spirit. And oh, how these men were changed! No longer timid and hiding in fear, they went out and Peter boldly preached the gospel. At the end of his message, after people asked what they must do to be saved, Peter said, *"Repent, and be baptized every one of you in the name of Jesus Christ for the remission of sins, and ye shall receive the gift of the Holy Ghost."* (Acts 2:1-38)

Notice there are two actions Peter cited as necessary before they could receive *"the gift of the Holy Ghost."*

First, they had to "repent." That word is *metanoeo* in Greek and has a slightly different meaning than the word used when John the Baptist told people to "repent." It does mean "to think differently". But it also means "to reconsider, transform, transfigure." Peter was saying, "now that you have heard that Jesus is the only one who can save you, that He is both Messiah and Lord, and has risen from the dead, reconsider your former position on how to be saved, and be transformed." In other words, instead of not believing on Jesus, now believe on Him; become transformed, become a new person in the process, and **then** be baptized.

So, first we believe that Jesus is our Savior, then we are baptized. Why? Because this baptism is symbolic and not a ritual cleansing. Our baptism symbolizes our identification with Jesus' death and resurrection. By submerging in water as though it were a grave, we, too, indicate our willingness to die to self then rise to a new, resurrected life in Christ. Then after this, we receive the gift of the Holy Ghost. In essence, baptism is an outward sign of an inner action.

Colossians 2:12 also affirms this. "(You, the believer, are) ***Buried*** *with him* (Jesus) *in baptism, wherein also ye are* ***risen*** *with him, through the faith of the operation of God who hath raised him from the dead."* Romans 6:4

adds this, *"Therefore we are **buried** with him* (Jesus) *by baptism into death: that like as Christ was **raised** up from the dead by the glory of the Father, even so we also should walk in newness of life."* Notice the theme: buried then raised. Again, our baptism symbolizes we, that is our selfish, sin nature, has died with Jesus and we are now resurrected with Him as a new person and into a new life. How wonderful is that! Our old sin nature is dead, and we can now live a new, powerful, holy life because we are in Christ and He is in us!

However, baptism does not save us.

Baptism cannot save us or cleanse us from sin. Only the blood of Jesus can do that. Some people use John 3:5 to claim that we must be baptized in order to be saved. This is an incorrect understanding of the Scripture.

Let's look at it: *"Jesus answered, Verily, verily, I say unto thee, expect a man be born of water and of the Spirit, he cannot enter into the kingdom of God."* That word born is *gennao* and means to procreate, bear, beget. In other words, it first indicates a physical birth. And that word "water" is *hudor*, the same word John the Baptist used, but has a double meaning, a play on words, if you will. It also refers to physical water that is broken during a physical birth as well as alluding to the water/rain of the Holy Spirit. But in addition to being born physically, we must also be born spiritually, by the power of the Holy Spirit. And "kingdom" is *basileia,* meaning "royalty, ruler, realm, foundation of power."

Putting it all together, it means that we are born physically through a flood of water because before a woman gives birth, her water breaks. But unless we accept Jesus as our Savior, die to self and are resurrected in new life with Christ (symbolized by water baptism) by the power of the Holy Spirit, in other words, be spiritually reborn or born again, we will not enter a foundation of power in God's realm.

Romans 6:6-8 explains it well. *"Knowing this, that our old man is crucified with him, that the body of sin might be destroyed that henceforth we should not serve sin. For he that is dead is free from sin. Now if we be dead with Christ, we believe that we shall also live with him."* Accepting Jesus and dying to self leads to living a powerful resurrection life in Christ. In Luke 24:49, before His ascension into heaven, Jesus tells his disciples, *"And behold, I send the promise of my Father upon you, but tarry ye in the city of Jerusalem until ye be endued with power from on high."* He's talking about the Holy Spirit. He's talking about power, God's power, that only the Holy Spirit can give us.

We need to live a powerful resurrected life in Christ, dead to self, and endued with the power of the Holy Spirit in order to enter a foundation of power in God's realm/kingdom so we can tread on *"serpents, and scorpions, and over all the power of the enemy."* (Luke 10:19)

In Mark 16:16 Jesus said, *"He that believeth and is baptized shall be saved; but he that believeth not shall be damned."* Notice the word "believeth" is mentioned first, showing the order of importance. Also note, he who is damned is the one who doesn't believe; not someone who isn't baptized.

Though infant baptism is practiced in some churches, it should more accurately be called a "dedication" to celebrate the time when a family dedicates their newborn to God. True baptism must be an act of free-will and only done after we have accepted Jesus as our Savior. The very act acknowledges that we are one with Christ and that we identify with both His death and resurrection, meaning, again, that we are prepared to die to self and live as Christ lived. And no baby can do that.

Why was infant baptism begun in the Church? It wasn't at first. Origen (185-254 A.D.) is the first to explicitly mention it in his writings, and Tertullian, writing between 198-203 A.D., claimed it was "common" practice. But it wasn't until the 3rd Century that infant baptism became "standard" practice. The Church was growing, and many areas didn't have a priest. The only priest some people saw was the one who came infrequently to do weddings, baptisms, etcetera. Parents began to fear their children might die in the meantime, and then what? Would they go to hell? So, because more and more people wanted their infants or young children baptized, it became first a tradition, then an official doctrine and sacrament of the Catholic Church.

Conclusion:

So, should a new believer in Christ be baptized, even if that person has been baptized as an infant? Yes. Again, this is because baptism, to mean anything at all, **must** be an act of free-will. And it **must** follow a free-will acceptance of Jesus as Lord and Savior. Also, Jesus Himself said we should be baptized (Mark 16:16).

Before Jesus returned to heaven He also instructed His disciples in Matthew 28:19 to, *"Go ye therefore, and teach all nations, baptizing them in the name of the Father, and of the Son, and of the Holy Ghost,"* indicating that He thought baptism was important. And if He thought it was important, so should we.

Question Three: *Who is the Holy Spirit?*

"And why is He important to a Christian?"

We first meet the Holy Spirit in Genesis 1:2b *"And the Spirit of God moved upon the face of the waters."* That word "moved" in Hebrew is *rachaph* and means "to brood." Webster defines brood "to sit on and hatch, to hover over, protect." So, we see that the Holy Spirit had a part in creation and restoration. He protected it. He hovered over it.

We meet the Holy Spirit again in Genesis 1:26. *"And God said, let* ***us*** *make man in* ***our*** *image, after* ***our*** *likeness."* This is the triune God, discussing the creation of man.

When Jesus, in Matthew 28:19 said, *"Go ye therefore, and teach all nations, baptizing them in the name of the Father, and of the Son, and of the Holy Ghost* (Spirit)*,"* He is referring to and naming the Trinity. He is stating that the Godhead is made up of God the Father, God the Son and God the Holy Ghost (Spirit). 1 John 5:7 gives further clarification: *"For* *there are three that bear record in heaven, the Father, The Word* (Jesus), *and the Holy Ghost* (Spirit, which is Jesus' Spirit) *and these three are **one**."* One God, three distinct persons.

So, we see that the Holy Spirit is the third Person in the Trinity. Yes, He is an actual person—not a force, not some cosmic gas or entity, but a person—One we can, according to Ephesians 4:30, actually grieve, upset and sadden.

1 Thessalonians 5:23 says, *"and I pray God your whole spirit and soul and body be preserved blameless unto the coming of our Lord Jesus Christ."*

Like the triune God, man is also triune. Nothing is wasted in the Bible. Here we learn not only that man is three-part, but the order of importance in God's estimation. First, the spirit (the spirit man) then the soul. That word "soul" in Greek is *psuche* from which we get the words psyche and psychology. It's our mind, our emotions, our personality. And finally, the body. We often reverse these and put the body first in importance rather than the spirit.

Old Testament references to God's Spirit:

In the Old Testament, God's Spirit came upon people rather than indwelled them. Number 11:25

says that God's Spirit, *"rested upon them,"* referring to the seventy elders who were given a portion of Moses' anointing.

Judges 3:10 says, regarding Caleb's younger brother, that *"the spirit of the Lord came upon him."* We see this same thing in Judges 6:34, *"the Spirit of the Lord came upon Gideon,"* in Judges 14:6 regarding Samson, *"and the Spirit of the Lord came mightily upon him,"* and in 1 Samuel 16:13 which after Samuel anointed David with oil, says that, *"the Spirit of the Lord came upon David from that day forward."* There are other examples, but those cited above should be enough to see that in the Old Testament, the Spirit of God rested upon certain people rather than indwelled them.

Then came Pentecost (Act 2:1-42)

and everything changed. Before Jesus returned to heaven, He promised His disciples that He'd send the Holy Spirit (John 7:39). At the appointed time, the Holy Spirit came as a strong wind (a breath) and tongues of fire (fury, fire, specifically—lightning). And the apostles, who, up until then had been hiding in fear, suddenly became fearless. They were so bold, in fact, that Peter's daring teaching won 3000 people to Jesus that same day.

Jewish scholars claim that when Moses received the law from God, it was the day of Pentecost or Feast of Weeks. The word "Pentecost" means "fifty." It was so named in the Old Testament because it fell on the fiftieth day after Passover. It was also called "feast of ingathering" and "feast of harvest." And in the New Testament, the spiritual significance is clear. It was the beginning of the harvest of souls into the Kingdom of God.

It's also interesting to note that on Pentecost, when Moses, after receiving the law, returned and found people worshipping the golden calf, ordered the people be punished and 3000 died, all slain by the sword. Romans 4:15 tells us that, *"the law worketh wrath,"* indicating that under the law you die because of your sins. But after the Holy Spirit came on Pentecost, 3000 people were saved, heralding the New Covenant and the age of grace.

Romans 8:2 says, *"For the law of the Spirit of life in Christ Jesus hath made me free from the law of sin and death."* Amen!

The purpose of the Holy Spirit:

The Holy Spirit is our helper, our teacher, our comforter, and revealer of truth. John 14:16-17 says, *"I will pray* (ask) *the Father, and He shall give you another* ***Comforter****, that he may abide with you for ever; Even the Spirit of* ***truth****; whom the world cannot receive, because it seeth him not, neither knoweth him: but ye know him; for he dwelleth with you, and shall be in you."* Wow! What a blessing to have Him in our lives!

I Corinthians 2:12-13 says, *"Now we have received not the spirit of the world, but the Spirit which is of God; that we might know the things that are freely given to us of God. Which things also we speak, not in the words which man's wisdom teacheth, but which the Holy Ghost* ***teaches****, comparing spiritual things with spiritual."* And what a kind and gentle teacher His is!

So, the Holy Spirit teaches us the things of God and helps us understand them. He also testifies of Jesus (John 15:26) and if that weren't enough, He guides us into all truth (John 16:13).

Next, the Holy Spirit makes us holy. 1 Peter 1:2 (Amplified Bible) *"You were chosen according to the purpose of God the Father, and were made a* ***holy*** *people by His Spirit, to obey Jesus Christ and be purified by His blood."* The Holy Spirit will convict us of any wrongdoing by pricking our conscience. Anyone who has ever had their conscience pricked knows it's an uncomfortable feeling. And it usually won't lift unless our offense has been dealt with.

The Holy Spirit also shows us how to serve God. Jesus' main concern and priority was to do the *"will of the Father."* In Acts 8:26-39 we read an unusual story that illustrates to what lengths the Holy Spirit may go in order to bring about the will of God through those who are submitted vessels. In these verses, Phillip is told by an angel to go to the Gaza desert where he finds an Ethiopian eunuch reading Isaiah. That's when the Holy Spirit instructs Phillip to speak to the man and explain how this Isaiah passage referred to Jesus. After the eunuch accepts and believes it, Phillip baptizes him and then the Holy Spirit immediately transports Phillip bodily to the city of Azotus (Ashdod).

Another amazing story is found in Acts 10:9-48 where Peter is given a vision of unclean and clean animals, and told by God (Holy Spirit) to no longer call those formerly unclean things "unclean" because they had been called clean by God. It was all in order to prepare Peter for his three visitors who waited downstairs to ask him to come to Cornelius' house, an unclean Gentile. To enter such a house would be unthinkable for a Jew but this story shows how easily the Holy Spirit can change a heart. Peter did go, and Cornelius' family and close friends came to the Lord. What a gracious God we serve! He desires all to come to Him.

While we may never experience anything as dramatic as the two stories mentioned, rest assured the Holy Spirit will guide and direct us in our day to day lives, if we let Him.

Years ago, I worked with a beautiful Christian woman who, in order to protect her privacy, I'll call Anna. This is the story she shared with me. Out of the blue, the Holy Spirit prompted her to make an afghan for a neighbor she hardly knew. He even told her the colors she was to use. She thought it a strange request, but out of a habit of obedience, she did it. When it was finished, Anna wrapped it up like a gift and brought it to the neighbor's house. After seeing no one was home, she left it on the doorstep with a note.

That evening, she got a call from the neighbor who was in tears. The afghan, its color and size, was exactly like the one her grandmother had made for her. It was a cherished gift and had recently been destroyed in a fire. "How could Anna have possibly known and created it in such detail?" the neighbor kept asking. Since it was late, Anna promised to visit her the next day.

Over coffee, the neighbor listened, in amazement, as Anna explained how God had instructed her to make the afghan. Not being a believer, the neighbor began asking Anna about her faith and was so captivated, that at the end of the visit she asked Anna if she'd come and do a Bible study for her and her family. Anna gladly agreed.

That one Bible study stretched into many. For months, Anna faithfully shared God's Word. It turned out that the neighbor had terminal cancer and hadn't long to live. But just before she died, Anna had the pleasure and privilege of leading her and her entire family to the Lord!

There is no limit to what the Holy Spirit can accomplish through a willing vessel!

Another function of the Holy Spirit is to enable us to worship God. Jesus said in John 4:23-24, *"But the time cometh, and now is, when the true worshippers shall worship the Father in spirit and in truth: for the Father seeketh such to worship him. God is a Spirit: and they that worship him must worship him in spirit and in truth."* All true worship must be spirit to Spirit, our spirit to God's spirit. It happens when our love for Him rises up in our hearts and causes our born-again spirits to connect with His.

In addition, the Holy Spirit seals us. Ephesians 1:13b-14 says that after hearing and believing the Gospel, *"ye were sealed with that holy Spirit of promise,*

Which is the earnest of our inheritance until the redemption of the purchased possession unto the praise of his glory." God puts His stamp of ownership, His seal, on us until we, the purchased possession (who are purchased by His blood) are safely home with Him. The Holy Spirit is the guarantee that we will receive what God has promised in His Word.

As mentioned earlier, we can grieve the Holy Spirit. Ephesians 4:30 tells us we shouldn't do this because the Holy Spirit is God's mark (seal) of ownership on us. Galatians 4:6-7 also says, *"And because ye are sons, God hath sent forth the Spirit of his Son* (the Holy Spirit) *into your hearts, crying, Abba, Father. Wherefore thou art no more a servant, but a son; and if a son, then an heir of God through Christ."* Because God has given us His Spirit, it testifies that we are not only His "purchased possession" but His son/daughter, His child, His heir! Think about that! God is saying that all that is His is now ours! That's how much He loves us and wants us to be part of His glorious eternity.

Romans 8:15-17 further confirms this by saying, *"For ye have not received the spirit of bondage again to fear; but ye have received the Spirit of adoption, whereby we cay Abba Father. The Spirit itself beareth witness with our spirit, that we are the children of God and if children, then heirs; heirs of God and joint heirs with Christ."*

Next, the Holy Spirit makes us His temple. God actually indwells us! Can it get any better? Again, this is so different from the Old Testament when God only came **upon** certain people. 1 Corinthians 3:16-17 says, *"Know ye not that ye are the temple of God, and that the Spirit of God dwelleth in you? If any man defile the temple of God, him shall God* ***destroy****; for the temple of God is holy, which temple ye are."* God takes this seriously. Notice that God warns He will destroy those who defile His temple. It makes me think of all the persecuted and martyred Christians around the world. It makes me think of all the innocent young children who pray to God in simple faith and who are abused by adults. Make no mistake. God sees it all.

But the good news is that because we are indeed the temple of God, the veil between the Holy of Holies and God has been torn. No longer are there barriers between God and us. And because we have become His temple, His residing place, we can understand why things like fornication, drunkenness and gluttony are sins. They defile God's temple. We have become the Holy of Holies where God's presence dwells. Are you beginning to see the position you hold as a spirit-filled child of God?

The Holy Spirit also empowers us so we can live full, victorious lives. Without Him, it would be impossible. In Ephesians 3:16-19, Paul prayed that God would, *"grant you* (the believer) *according to the riches of his glory, to be* ***strengthened*** *with might by his Spirit in the inner man; That Christ may dwell in your hearts by faith; that ye, being rooted and grounded in love, Many be able to comprehend with all saints what is the breadth, and length, and depth , and height; And to know the love of Christ, which passeth knowledge, that ye might be* ***filled*** *with all the fulness of God."* So, not only does the Holy Spirit strengthen us, but He fills us with knowledge, especially the knowledge that we are LOVED. Oh, how the world needs that. There's not one person on the face of the earth who doesn't want to be loved. And to be loved by God . . . well, nothing can compare with that.

And finally, the Holy Spirit makes us one body-the Body of Christ. 1 Corinthians 12:13 says, *"For by one Spirit are we all baptized into one body, whether we be Jews or Gentiles, whether we be bond* (slave) *or free."* Ephesians 4:4 also confirms this, *"there is one body and one Spirit."* As believers, we are all one in Christ, no matter what church we go to.

What about the fruit of the Spirit?

Galatians 5:22-23 tells us this: *"But the fruit of the Spirit is love, joy, peace, longsuffering* (patience), *gentleness, goodness, faith, Meekness, temperance* (self-control)." If we want to be more loving, joyful, peaceful, etcetera, then we need to yield to the Holy Spirit and ask Him to work these things into our lives.

The Holy Spirit also gives us gifts.

1 Corinthians 12:7-10 lists them: word of wisdom, word of knowledge, faith, gifts of healing, working of miracles, prophecy, discerning of spirits, tongues, interpretation of tongues.

A brief description follows:

The word of wisdom is speaking the right thing at the right time into a person's life or situation, and it is Godly wisdom not man's wisdom or the wisdom of the world.

A word of knowledge is supernaturally knowing something about a person or situation that you would not otherwise know, and which knowledge comes from God.

Faith, here, is referring to supernatural faith. It's extraordinary faith that God may give someone during extraordinary times. An example would be God asking someone of modest means to build a large complex like a school or orphanage, and the person doing so strictly by faith.

The gift of healing: All believers are called to *"lay hands on the sick, and they shall recover"* because that's what Jesus said in Mark 16:18b. But the gift of healing is something different. This is an anointing you see on those with healing ministries where hundreds, sometimes thousands, come to a healing service and multitudes are healed.

The working of miracles is different from the gift of healing. A healing may not always manifest immediately. It could take days, sometimes longer. But a miracle is something immediately visible such as a person growing a new leg where there was none before or someone being raised from the dead.

Prophecy is a declaration, a Divine revelation or message from God to warn, to inspire, to encourage or uplift the hearer/s.

Discerning of spirits is knowing, and sometimes seeing, the spirits that are tormenting a person or are causing a negative situation. Often it goes hand-in-hand with a deliverance ministry, but it doesn't have to.

The gift of tongues is where I'll spend a bit more time because it's so maligned in many quarters and so important to the Body of Christ. There are two types of tongues:

The 1st type

we see in Romans 8:26-27. *"Likewise the Spirit also helpeth our infirmities* (weaknesses)*: for we know not what we should pray for as we ought: but the Spirit itself maketh intercession for us with groanings which cannot be uttered. And he that searcheth the hearts knoweth what is the mind of the Spirit, because he maketh intercession for the saints according to the will of God."*

Here, we pray along with the Holy Spirit, and most of the time don't know what we're praying. Rather, we are praying what's on His heart and according to His knowledge of that person or situation. Even so, we have complete control. We can pray at will and stop at will. I find praying in tongues an incredible tool, especially when I don't know how or what to pray for.

1 Corinthians 14:2, *"for he that speaketh in an unknown tongue speaketh not unto men but unto God, for no man understandeth him, howbeit in the spirit he speaketh mysteries."* This is a time when God, through His Holy Spirit, can reveal things to us; things not

formerly understood. This can include answers to questions long held.

Praying in tongues also edifies the person praying. 1 Corinthians 14:4 says, *"he that speaketh in an unknown tongue edifieth himself."* That word edify means to "be a house builder, construct, embolden." So, when we pray in tongues, we build ourselves up, we embolden ourselves.

And here is where **interpretation of tongues** comes in. Sometimes a person will be led to give a brief public monologue in tongues and when that happens, if it's authentic, there should always be an interpretation of that monologue. In other words, God should give someone in the group knowledge of what was just said.

The thing is, we don't have to speak in tongue, but we have the privilege of doing so.

The 2nd type

we see in Acts 2:4, *"and they were all filled with the Holy Ghost, and began to speak with other tongues, as the Spirit gave them utterance."* This type was manifested at Pentecost when the apostles began speaking in foreign languages that were understood by the people around them. I've never experience this but have heard of evangelists or ministers who prayed in tongues during a service in a foreign land and was completely understood because, unbeknown to them, they spoke in the language of that country, without ever having learned it.

Receiving the Baptism of the Holy Spirit:

In the early church (the first 500 years) there were two baptisms **after** salvation. The first was water baptism and the second, the baptism of the Holy Spirit. These followed immediately after a person came to Christ. Acts 2:38, *"Then Peter said unto them,* ***Repent*** *and* ***be baptized*** (water baptism) *every one of you in the name of Jesus Christ for the remission of sins and ye shall receive the* ***gift of the Holy Ghost*** (the baptism of the Holy Spirit)*."*

Again, notice that the word "repent" comes before "be baptized." Peter had just finished telling the crowd on Pentecost about Jesus. At the end of his teaching, in verse 37, it says that the people were *"pricked in their heart, and said unto Peter and to the rest of the apostles, Men and brethren, what shall we do* (to be saved)*?"* In response, Peter tells them to change their view and accept God's will for salvation (Jesus); in other words, "repent" then be baptized both by water and the Holy Spirit.

The baptism of the Holy Spirit has, in many churches, become confirmation. But scripturally speaking, both baptisms, that of water and the Spirit, should come soon after salvation.

So, how do we receive the baptism of the Holy Spirit? Luke 11:13 says, *"if ye then, being evil, know how to give good gifts unto your children: how much more shall your heavenly Father give the Holy Spirit to them that* ***ask*** *Him?"* And Galatians 3:14b tells us that because Jesus suffered and died for us, we Gentiles can also inherit the blessings promised to Abraham, and that *"we might receive the promise of the Spirit through* ***faith****."*

So, we received the Holy Spirit by doing two things: first by **asking**, then by **believing** we have received Him. Feelings don't count. We don't need goosebumps or our hair standing on end to insure we have received the Holy Spirit. We simply ask and believe.

But did you know there is a difference between receiving the Holy Spirit upon salvation—which everyone who accepts Jesus as Savior receives—and receiving the baptism of the Holy Spirit of fire? When Jesus first appeared to His apostles in the upper room after the resurrection, John 20:21-22 says, *"then said Jesus to them again, Peace be unto you:*

as my Father hath sent me, even so send I you. And when he had said this, he breathed on them, and saith unto them, Receive ye the Holy Ghost." Here the disciples, as believers in Jesus and the New Covenant, received the Holy Spirit before Pentecost.

Yet, Jesus tells them to tarry in Jerusalem and wait for the Holy Spirit. Acts 1:4-5 says, *"and being assembled together with them,* (Jesus) *commanded them that they should not depart from Jerusalem, but wait for the promise of the Father, which, saith he, ye have heard of me. For John truly baptized with water, but ye shall be baptized with the Holy Ghost not many days hence."* Acts 1:8 goes on to say, *"But ye shall receive power, after that the Holy Ghost is come upon you, and ye shall be witnesses unto me both in Jerusalem, and in all Judea, and in Samaria, and unto the uttermost part of the earth."*

Why two impartations of the Holy Spirit? When Jesus breathed on His disciples and said, *"receive the Holy Spirit,"* He was sealing them. Remember Ephesians 1:13-14? It told us that God puts His stamp (His seal) of ownership on us by giving us the Holy Spirit. In the same manner, when we accept Jesus, we, too, are sealed with Holy Spirit just like when Jesus breathe on His disciples.

But the actual baptism of the Holy Spirit is when the Holy Spirit infuses us with power and fire. We may not see flaming tongues or lightening as on the day of Pentecost, but this baptism is just as real, just as powerful. There was a **big** difference in the disciples between John 20:21-22 (when Jesus breathed on them) and Acts 2:1-4 (when the Holy Spirit fell on them with fire and power), just as there will be in us.

The Outpouring of the Holy Spirit in the last days.

Joel 2:28-30 says, *"And it shall come to pass afterward that I* (God) *will pour out my spirit upon all flesh; and your sons and your daughters shall prophesy, your old men shall dream dreams, your young men shall see visions: And also upon the servants and upon the handmaids in those days will I pour out my spirit. And I will shew wonders in the heavens and in the earth, blood, and fire, and pillars of smoke."*

This is repeated in Acts 2:17-19. *"And it shall come to pass* ***in the last days****, saith God, I will pour out of my Spirit upon all flesh: and your sons and your daughters shall prophesy, and your young men shall see visions, and your old men shall dream dreams: And on my servants and on my handmaidens I will pour out in those days of my Spirit; and they shall prophesy: and I will shew wonders in heaven above, and signs in the earth beneath; blood and fire, and vapour of smoke."*

But just before, in verse 16, it says, regarding the apostles and Pentecost and what happened with the infilling of the Holy Spirit, *"But this is that which was spoken by the prophet Joe,"* indicating that the "former" rain had taken place in the Upper Room. But the Bible doesn't just talk about the former rain of the Holy Spirit, but a latter rain as well (Hosea 6:3; James 5:7). And the latter rain will be more powerful than the former. And it will occur in the *"last days."*

We are certainly in the *"last days"* and will see more and more of the signs and wonders both Joel and Luke wrote about. But as the move of the Holy Spirit increases and intensifies, so will Satan's. He will try to counterfeit the things of God and will eventually set up a One World Government complete with a satanic trinity: Satan (dragon), the beast (antichrist) and the false prophet.

There will also be a counterfeit Holy Spirit. The Holy Spirit gives us peace and joy, and sometimes His joy appears as a high (Acts 2:15). In that respect, Satan's counterfeit Holy Spirit is drugs. Four times, in the Book of Revelation (Rev 9:21; 18:23; 21:8; 22:15) when the word for "sorcery" is used, it's the Greek word *pharmakeas* from which we get the word "pharmacy." That word means "pharmacist, a druggist, a spell giving potion, a poisoner."

Revelation 18:23 says, speaking of the fall of Babylon, symbol of the corrupt world system ruled by the Satanic trinity, *"And the light of a candle shall shine no more at all in thee; and the voice of the bridegroom and of the bride shall be heard no more at all in thee: for thy merchants were the great men of the earth; for by thy* ***sorceries*** (by their *pharmakeas*, their drugs) *were all nations deceived."*

So, is the Holy Spirit important to a Christian and do we need His baptism?

Yes, on both counts. Why? So God can use us in these last days. So He can empower us to boldly finish our race. And whether that race is in our prayer closet or out on the streets witnessing to others, we need His empowering in order to truly be what God wants us to be. D.L. Moody, when asked why he constantly spoke about his need to be filled with the Holy Spirit said, "because I leak."

The world has a way of wearing us down. And sometimes we need a fresh touch of the Holy Spirit. Let's be all we can in Him!

PRAY for the baptism of the Holy Spirit.

If you've never been baptized in the Holy Spirit or if you feel a need for a new touch, a fresh touch—and we all do from time to time—pray this prayer:

Father God, You promised to give the Holy Spirit to those who ask. You are a good God and do all things well. I'm asking now for You to fill me or fill me afresh. I need Your touch, Your power. I need to be renewed so I can finish my race strong for You. Fill me with Your peace, Your joy, Your love. Make me more like You. I pray this all in Jesus' mighty name, Amen.

Question Four: *How can I increase my faith?*

"My faith seems puny. What can I do about it?"

I'm sure every believer, new or old, wants to be a powerhouse of faith, but sometimes, especially at the beginning of our faith walk, we just don't know how. And examples in the Bible, though uplifting, can leave one intimidated and wondering if great faith is only for the select few.

Noah built an ark just on God's say so, without ever having seen rain. Abraham left his family and country and headed for a new land but didn't know where. That's right, he didn't even know where he was going! He only knew, or rather believed, that God would continue to show him the way until he reached his destination. And then there's Moses, the superhero of faith. At his command, ten plagues were unleashed upon Egypt and the Red Sea parted. He also witnessed the destruction of the entire Egyptian army before guiding his flock, of millions, for forty years in the wilderness because God had promised to settle them in a land "flowing with milk and honey." And of course, there's Joshua. Who hasn't heard of the walls of Jericho and how they fell under his command after the Israelites marched around them for seven days?

Though they were real people, somehow they don't seem real. Instead, they seem larger-than-life; those you'd see on the big screen surrounded by plenty of special effects. How could we ever attain this kind of faith? Scripture says we can remove mountains but sometimes we can't even remove our heartburn. So . . . can we or can we not become people of great faith?

The resounding answer is, YES!

Hebrews 11:1 tells us, *"Now faith is the substance of things hoped for, the evidence of things not seen."* The key word is substance. It's *hupostasis* in Greek and means "in stanch confidence." In other words, faith is unshakable confidence in something we hope will happen but have no evidence it will. So, to be a person of faith we need to have a strong or stanch, unwavering hope in what we are believing for.

Still . . . how do we get this faith; this strong unwavering hope?

The Bible tells us in Romans 10:17. *"So then faith cometh by hearing, and hearing by the word of God."*

This clearly tells us that the Word of God is key to increasing our faith. We must get to know it, because the more we know the Word, the more we understand who God is and the more we can trust Him. Jesus is the Word made flesh. When we know the Word, we know Him. And we slowly begin to fall in love with Him and understand that He loves us, too, and only wants what's best for us. We begin to see that God is for us and not against us. We see His faithfulness through His actions with others. And we learn that God is no respecter of persons, which means we can count on Him doing these same things for us. We begin to understand that God delivers what He promises, and He does all things well, though not always according to our way of thinking.

All of God's promises are obtained by faith and obedience. Did you know that, according to Hebrews 11:6, without faith it's impossible to please God? As previously mentioned, building our faith is an on-going process. It doesn't happen overnight. We need to build a foundation. Then we start trusting God in the little things and before we know it, we are trusting Him in bigger things. If we don't have faith that God will heal heartburn, how can we have faith that He will heal cancer?

What else does the Bible say about faith?

I think the apostles struggled like we do. They saw Jesus perform many miracles yet still had trouble believing Him at times. Look what happened when they tried crossing the Sea of Galilee in a storm. According to Mark 4:35-40, the wind and waves rocked the boat and nearly flooded it. They were terrified and woke Jesus, who had been peacefully sleeping in the back. *"Master, carest thou not that we perish?"* they shouted above the roar of the waves. You can hear both fear and indignation in their voice. *Don't you care about* ***us****? Any minute we are going to die!* was what they were really saying. Did they actually believe Jesus would let anything happen to them, especially while HE was in the boat?

And how about the time they questioned Jesus' ability to feed four thousand with only seven loaves and fishes (Matthew 15:32-38) after they had already seen Him feed five thousand with just five loaves and two fishes (Matthew 14:16-21).

And then there's this: after Jesus resurrected from the dead and appeared to the disciples, Thomas, the one who missed it all, said, *"Except I shall see in his hands the print of the nails, and put my finger into the print of the nails and thrust my hand into his side, I will not believe."* (John 20:24-25)

It makes Thomas sound pitiful. But haven't many of us been there, in situations where we've said, "Don't you care about me, Lord?" Or, "Unless I see a certain thing with my own eyes, I can't accept it, I won't believe it."

Perhaps that's why the apostles said, in Luke 17:5-6, *"Lord, Increase our faith. And the Lord said, If ye had faith as a grain of mustard seed, ye might say unto this sycamine tree, be thou plucked up by the root, and be thou planted in the sea; and it should obey you."*

Jesus basically repeated this in Matthew 17:20, *"If you have faith as a grain of mustard seed ye shall say unto this Mountain, Remove hence to yonder place; and it shall remove; and nothing shall be impossible unto you."*

How big is a mustard seed? Wikipedia says it's one to two millimeters in size or 0.039 to 0.079 inches. That tells me that even a little faith can accomplish much. Romans 12:3b also says, *"God has dealt to every man the measure of faith,"* implying we all have some faith implanted in us by God. If so, our job is to nurture it, feed it and let it grow.

And that's where learning Scripture comes in. When we read about the things Jesus did for others, we start believing He will do the same for us, and our faith seed begins to grow.

I like the story of the woman with a hemorrhage. She had been bleeding for twelve years; had spent all her money on doctors and had only gotten worse. She heard about Jesus, about His miracles. And that's what she needed. A miracle. He was her last hope. *If only she could touch the hem of His garment.* But her bleeding made her unclean. To touch a rabbi in such a condition was a serious offense. What would happen if someone called her on it? But twelve years of suffering made her desperate. In fear and trembling, she reached out and connected with Jesus. And instantly, she was healed! But when Jesus turned, looking for the person who caused virtue to drain from Him, there was nothing left for her to do but fall at His feet and confess. And then Jesus responded, *"Daughter, be of good comfort; they faith hath made thee whole."* (Matthew 9:22; Mark 5:25-34; Luke 8:43-48)

Oh, how this touches my heart! How tender and compassionate is our Jesus! He didn't rebuke her. He didn't tell her that, being both unclean and a woman, she should never have touched Him. He just loved her and healed her.

Can faith make us whole, too? Yes. Jesus paid for every sickness and disease on planet earth, and it's by faith that we appropriate our healing. But notice, the women was convinced she would be healed by touching Jesus. She never wavered or doubted. Her faith was strong. It had to be for her to have the courage to violate her culture's protocol. In like manner, we cannot waver either.

James 1:6-7 tells us the consequence of wavering. *"But let him ask in faith, nothing wavering. For he that wavereth is like a wave of the sea driven with the wind and tossed.* ***For let not that man think that he shall receive anything of the Lord."***

Wavering in our faith, going back and forth thinking yes, God will do it, no God won't, but then again maybe He will, gets us nothing. Zippo. Zilch. Again, that's why we need to understand Who God is, what His Word says, and His will for our life. Then we can ask in confidence and faith. Then we will receive.

Did you know that, *"whatsoever is not of faith is sin"*? That's what Romans 14:23b says. Why? Because the opposite of faith is doubt, and that means doubting God; what He says; what He is capable of; and doubting His incredible goodness. Jesus actually rebuked His disciples for their lack of faith (Matthew 6:30; Matthew 8:26; Matthew 14:31).

The Israelites serve as a good object lesson. Lack of faith made them wander in the desert for forty years. If only they had believed God and not doubted, they would have entered the promised land four decades earlier (see Numbers 13:1-33; 14:1-38). It's the same for us. Doubt will cause us to wander in our wilderness, while faith will bring us to our promised land.

When my son was young, he developed a bone infection in his heel and had to be hospitalized and given massive doses of antibiotics, intravenously. His pediatrician said he'd never walk normally again. Those words drove me to my knees. And after a flood of tears and deep intercession, God gave me a vision of him running and jumping. That's when my faith kicked in. That's when I dried my eyes and began praising God for healing my son. And he *was* healed. And he *did* walk normally.

Sometimes, we need to get a specific word from God in order to walk by faith through those rough patches in our life. But once He gives it, we need to stand on it and believe He will bring it about even when we don't see any immediate results. My son was hospitalized for almost two weeks, and during that time I never saw any indication that God's Word was manifesting. It was only after he got home that I saw God's promise unfold.

How did I have faith for this? It was years in the making. I always believed God capable of doing great miracles, even in this day and age. For me, it was never could God do it? The sticking point was always, will He do it for *me*? My time in the Word gradually made me see and understand God's great love for each one of us, individually, even though no one is worthy of such love. But it doesn't come down to our worth. It comes down to Who God is, and to His love. And yes, what God did for someone else, God can and will do for you.

God is no respecter of persons.

Oh, there are so many stories in the Bible that should lift our faith! Luke 7:50 talks about the woman with the alabaster jar, how Jesus forgave her sins and said, *"Thy **faith** hath saved thee; go in peace."* And in Luke 18:42, a blind beggar cries out to Jesus for mercy. Jesus asks him what he wants, and the beggar says, *"Lord, that I may receive my sight."* Jesus responds, *"Receive thy sight; thy **faith** hath saved thee."* And in Acts 3:16, Peter cures a lame man and tells the crowd that it was **faith** in the name of Jesus that healed the man. And doesn't James 5:15 tells us that, *"the prayer of* ***faith*** *shall save the sick"*?

God is no respecter of persons.

The thing is, we must believe it before we see it. II Corinthians 5:7 tells us we are to walk by faith and not by sight, meaning we don't go by what we see or even feel. We go by what the Word of God says. And Hebrews 6:12 says, *"That ye be not slothful, but followers of them who through faith and patience inherit the promises."*

That's how we do it. We build our faith through the Word. We don't look at our circumstances. And we wait patiently for God to act. Remember, His timing is perfect.

Some other Scriptures to consider:

- II Corinthians 1:24b, *"for by* ***faith*** *ye stand."*
- Romans 1:17; Galatians 3:11; Hebrews 10:38; Habakkuk 2:4b, *"the just shall live by his* ***faith****."*
- Hebrews 11:33, *"Who through* ***faith*** *subdued kingdoms, wrought righteousness, obtained promises, stopped the mouths of lions."*

- Galatians 3:7, *"Know ye therefore that they which are of **faith**, the same are the children of Abraham."*
- James 1:3, *"Knowing this, that the trying of your **faith** worketh patience."*
- 1 Peter 1:7, *"That the trial of your **faith**, being much more precious than of gold that perisheth, though it be tried with fire, might be found unto praise and honour and glory at the appearing of Jesus Christ."*
- Jude 20, *"But ye, beloved, building up your most holy **faith**, praying in the Holy Ghost."*

There is much to unpack in these Scriptures, but I'll only skim the surface. They tell us that it's faith that enables us to stand, to be the Christian God wants us to be; to face those giants in our lives and overcome and appropriate God's promises. And because we are "the just, the holy and innocent," which is what that word "just" in Romans 1:17 means in Greek, we are to live by faith. That's our modus operandi. That should be our normal way of doing things. That's how we subdue kingdoms (the devil's domain). Our faith also enables us to inherit all the promises given to Abraham! And when our faith is tried, God is working patience in us. God values our faith. To Him, it is more precious than gold, and it is holy. Also, we can build up our faith by praying in tongues.

And here's more good news. Hebrews 12:2a says, *"Looking unto Jesus the author and finisher of our faith."* So, who implants faith in us and nurtures it so it can grow? JESUS! We are His workmanship, and if we get into His Word, He will see to it that it will not return void, and that it builds up our faith. What a wonderful God we serve! He does the heavy lifting, while we reap the benefits!

But a cautionary note: Our faith in never in our faith. Our faith is in God. 1 Peter 1:21 confirms this. *"Who by him do believe in God, that raised him up from the dead, and gave him glory;* ***that your faith and hope might be in God."***

Conclusion:

Remember, *"without faith it is impossible to please God,"* so it's important that we get this right. At the same time, we need to understand Isaiah 55:8-9, *"For my thoughts are not your thoughts, neither are your ways my ways, saith the LORD. For as the heavens are higher than the earth so are my ways higher than your ways, and my thoughts than your thoughts."*

God is not always going to act the way we think He should. Nor will we always clearly see the way forward, as Moses did, when God gave him specific instructions. More often it will be like Abraham, who was told to "go" but not told where. That's the one-foot-in-front-of-the-other instruction, the kind where God reveals only one step at a time. But it's not scary if we truly believe Romans 8:28, that *"all things work together for good to them that love God, to them who are the called according to his purpose."* Or, if we believe that God will never leave us or forsake us (Hebrews 13:5) or that nothing can separate us from the love of God (Romans 8:35-39). Once these truths are firmly planted in our heart, then faith and the faith walk become an exciting adventure!

Question Five: *How do I pray?*

"I'm not very eloquent. What do I say?"

First, what is prayer?

Prayer is simply talking to God. And God can hear us whether we sit, kneel or stand. Some people even pray in the shower! And God isn't looking for eloquence. He's looking for sincerity. He sees the heart. And He knows what's in it.

In addition to sincerity, I believe we need to be respectful. Sometimes, when people speak about how they talk to God, it makes me cringe. Their tone is demanding and arrogant. We must always be mindful of Who we are talking to. Yes, God is our friend. But He's also the Creator of the universe, the King of kings and Lord of lords and the judge of all the earth. He's not an indentured servant we can order about nor is He Santa Clause, existing to gratify our every whim. So, when we pray, we should always incorporate these two elements: sincerity and reverence/respect.

When should we pray?

Jesus prayed often. He was always going off alone to pray and seek His Father's direction. And Paul, the apostle, who wrote so much of the New Testament, said, in Colossians 1:9, that he constantly prayed for those in the church. In I Thessalonians 5:17 he went on to tell us we should, *"pray without ceasing."* And in I Timothy 2:8 he said, *"I will therefore that men pray every where, lifting up holy hands, without wrath and doubting."*

If you read the history of almost any major ministry, you'll discover it was bathed in prayer long before its actual formation. And all major revivals were founded on prayer before God began to move. We can say that nothing important is accomplished without prayer.

So, when should we pray? I believe we should be in an attitude of prayer all the time. We live busy lives, with demanding jobs, houses to clean, children to tend, and a ton of other things to do. We can't be in our prayer closet all day. But we can be in an attitude of prayer, meaning when we are doing things like getting dressed or the dishes or driving, we can talk to God. There are many such prayer opportunities throughout the day. Even a one-second prayer like, "Jesus I love you," is meaningful. This constant attitude of prayer will get easier as we practice and discipline ourselves.

How do we pray?

Psalms 100:4 tells us to, *"Enter into his* (God's) *gates with thanksgiving, and into his courts with praise; be thankful unto him and bless his name."* Obviously, that is the proper place to start. We shouldn't approach God with a laundry list of things we want or feel we need. We should first begin by thanking Him for the things He has already done for us and praising Him for Who His is.

Also, the Holy Spirit will help us when we don't know how to pray. Romans 8:26 says, *"Likewise the Spirit also helpeth our infirmities; for we know not what we should pray for as we ought: but the Spirit itself maketh intercession for us with groanings which cannot be uttered."*

Of course, our hearts must be right toward God, as well as toward others, meaning we are not to harbor any grudges, resentments or unforgiveness toward anyone. We also need to bind the enemy before praying so he can't interfere or interject his thoughts or ideas. More about this in the section on spiritual warfare prayers.

In Matthew 6:5-13, Jesus gives us valuable prayer instructions. He tells us not to be like the hypocrites who do things for show or to appear "spiritual." He tells us that when we pray, we are to go into our closet, meaning a private place. In addition, we are not to pray vain, repetitious prayer. Again, this goes back to sincerity, back to sharing our heart with God and not just mouthing words.

In what has become known as the Lord's Prayer, Jesus gave us a wonderful example of prayer. Through it, Jesus tells us **how** to pray rather than what to pray. Though it's an amazing prayer, one I often pray, I don't believe Jesus ever meant for us to mindlessly recite it over and over as though it were a mantra.

However, there are important points in that prayer we need to take note of:

- *"Our Father Who is in heaven."* First, we need to acknowledge that God is our heavenly Father.
- *"Hallowed be thy name."* God is holy.
- *"Thy Kingdom come."* God has a kingdom and a kingdom agenda.
- *"Thy will be done as it is in heaven."* He wants His will to permeate the earth.
- *"Give us this day our daily bread."* God is interested in our needs, and it's perfectly correct to discuss them with Him.

- *"And forgive us our trespasses."* We need to acknowledge our sins and ask forgiveness.
- *"As we forgive those who trespass against us."* We are to freely forgive anyone who has wronged us and give up all grievances and grudges.
- *"Lead us not into temptation but deliver us from evil."* We ask Him to protect us.
- *"For Thine is the Kingdom and the power and the glory forever."* We acknowledge that it's all about Him—that He is everything.

It puts us in the right frame of mind regarding the proper way to speak to God, to acknowledge Who He is and to speak from our heart. And after we share with God, we listen. And God will respond. How? Sometimes we'll hear His voice. This has only happened to me, twice. More often, He'll bring a certain Scripture to mind or give me a sense of peace about the matter. Other times, thoughts or pictures may come to mind. Sometimes, I'll just know that I know that I know something. But it's all God speaking. He'll speak to each of us uniquely and in a way we can both receive and accept.

Next, we need to ask everything in Jesus' name. John 14:13-14 says, *"And whatsoever ye shall ask in my name, that will I do, that the Father may be glorified in the Son. If ye shall ask anything in my name, I will do it."* Then in John 16:23, Jesus says, *"and in that day* (after

He returns to the Father) *ye shall ask me nothing. Verily, verily, I say unto you, Whatsoever ye shall ask the Father in my name, he will give it you."*

God's heart regarding prayer:

Matthew 7:7-11 reveals God's heart as that of a "giving father." His desire is to give us good things. Romans 8:31-32 says, *"If God is for us who can be against us? He that spared not his own Son, but delivered Him up for us all, how shall he not with him also fully give us all things?"*

If God gave us Jesus, He'll give us anything else that's good for us. He not only wants to answer our prayers but delights in doing so. That doesn't mean He'll give us everything we ask for. Sometimes, what we want isn't what's best.

Factors that hinder our prayers:

In Deuteronomy 1:42-45 Moses tells the Israelites that because of their disobedience, God won't hear their prayers. In like manner, disobedience can hinder our prayers.

Unconfessed sin is another issue. Isaiah 59:2 says, *"But your iniquities have separated between you and your God, and your sins have hid his face from you, that he will not hear."* King David, in Psalm 66:18 said, *"If I regard iniquity in my heart, the Lord will not hear me."* And 1 Peter 3:12 further confirms this, *"For the eyes of the Lord are over the righteous and his ears are open unto their prayers, but the face of the Lord is against them that do evil."*

James 5:16 continues the theme. *"Confess your faults one to another and pray one for another, that ye may be healed. The effectual fervent prayers of a righteous man* ***availeth*** *much."* A righteous man is one covered by the blood of Jesus, one in right standing with God.

If we are gossiping or backbiting or causing strife and we don't confess these as sins and put them under the blood, we are not in right standing with God. We are saved, but our communion with God is impaired. And that word "availeth" in Greek is *ischuo* and means "be of strength, to have force." When we are in right standing with God, our prayers have strength and force. When we are not in right standing with Him, they don't.

Next, we must pray in faith. Matthew 21:22 says, *"And all things whatsoever ye shall ask in prayer,* ***believing****, ye shall receive."* And James 1:6-8 tells us what happens if we don't believe. *"But let him ask in faith, nothing wavering. For he that wavereth is like a wave of the sea driven with the wind and tossed. For let* *not that man think that he shall receive any thing of the Lord. A double minded man is unstable in all his ways."*

We are not to vacillate between believing God and not believing Him. We begin by trusting Him in little things. Then it will be easier to trust Him in the bigger ones. And we are not to condemn ourselves if we don't have the faith of Moses or Daniel. If we feel we need more faith we can get it, as explained in the chapter on faith.

James 4:2b-3 says, *"Ye have not because ye ask not. Ye ask and receive not because ye ask amiss that ye may consume it upon your lusts."* Here we have two more reasons for not receiving from God. We fail to ask Him. Or, we pray selfish prayers, prayers not according to His will. In other words, our motives are wrong.

Then there's the issue of timing. Timing is everything. And everything comes in God's good time which is always perfect. Romans 11:33 says, *"O the depth of the riches both of the wisdom and knowledge of God! How unsearchable are his judgments, and his ways past finding out!"* We need to trust God. We may not know what He's doing or why He's delaying the answer to our prayer, but He knows what's best.

How do we get our prayers answered?

According to 1 Peter 3:12, God will not hear our prayers if we do "evil." And if the Holy Spirit convicts us of doing any evil, I believe we must repent. Believers in hyper-grace will take exception to this. They'll say repentance is not necessary; that grace now covers every sin we have committed or ever will commit. That's true. Grace does cover them all. But when the Holy Spirit convicts us of something by pricking our conscience or bringing it to mind, we need to deal with it. Sometimes, He does this because He wants to adjust our wrong thinking or correct a destructive pattern in our life, and the first step is getting us to acknowledge it is wrong. I would never advise ignoring the Holy Spirit when He moves this way.

We also need to be obedient to God and His Word. And God said, in Jeremiah 29:13, *"And ye shall seek me* (God) *and find me, when ye shall search for me with all your heart."* So, here's the trio: we need to repent, be obedient and have a right heart attitude. These will give us an open heaven when we pray. It puts us in a position for God to be able to honor the words He spoke in Jeremiah 33:3, *"Call unto me, and I will answer thee, and shew thee great and mighty things, which thou knowest not."*

Matthew 6:25-33 is very revealing. It tells us that God knows our needs and we can trust Him to meet them. But that last verse, verse 33, zeros in on where our attention should be focused. *"Seek ye first the Kingdom of God and his righteousness and all these things shall be added unto you."* Our priorities should always be for the things of God. And if they are, then God will take care of our needs. And Jeremiah 29:11 assures us that God only wants what's good for us. *"For I know the thoughts that I think toward you, saith the LORD, thoughts of peace, and not of evil, to give you an expected end."*

In John 15:7 Jesus says, *"If ye abide in me and my words abide in you, ye shall ask what ye will and it shall be done unto you."* If we are really abiding in Jesus and His Word abides in us, then we are not going to ask amiss. Rather, we are going to care about the things God cares about. And we will ask according to His Word and therefore His will.

1 John 5:14-15 says, *"And this is the* ***confidence*** *that we have in him, that, if we ask anything according to his will, he heareth us. And if we know that he hears us, whatsoever we ask, we know that we have the petitions that we desire of him."* So, we are to ask confidently, according to His will, and then believe we will receive it.

We are also to pray diligently. Again, 1 Thessalonians 5:17 tells us we are to *"pray without ceasing."* David said in Ps 55:17, *"Evening, and morning, and at noon, will I pray, and cry aloud: and he shall hear my voice."* What David was saying is that he prayed all day long. Are we praying all day long? Or just sending out a quick text-like prayer? It makes a difference.

So, how do we get our prayers answered? We can glean seven basic necessary conditions from all the above:

1. We enter God's presence with thanksgiving and praise.
2. We come boldly without condemnation. We are not engaging in willful disobedience or sins. But if we have, these things have been confessed and put under the blood of Jesus.
3. Our relationships with those in our life are right. We hold no resentment, bitterness or anger toward anyone.
4. We pray with right motives and not selfish prayers for our own gratification.
5. We ask the Holy Spirit to help us pray.
6. We pray in the name of Jesus.
7. We are sincerely open to hearing God's will for us in this situation or issue, and willing to accept His will.

Types of Prayers:

Prayers of Petition: It's a request and is usually specific. This includes prayers for ourselves as well as others. Philippians 2:4 says, *"Look not every man on his own things, but every man also on the things of others."* In other words, we're not just to be concerned about ourselves. A good part of our prayer life should be devoted to praying for others.

But whether we are praying for ourselves or others, we need to ask the Holy Spirit for guidance and wisdom, which He will provide because He is our teacher. How valuable is this when a son or daughter is ready to find a life-partner, and we, as parents, pray for that right, godly spouse? How many mistakes and heartaches could be avoided if only we prayed before entering a marriage, a business partnership, a friendship, a move, a job, etcetera.

In addition, we are to pray for people we like and those we don't. In Matthew 5:44 Jesus says, *"But I say unto you, love your enemies, bless them that curse you, do good to them that hate you and* ***pray*** *for them which despitefully use you and persecute you."*

We are also to pray for our leaders, our government and our country. 2 Chronicles 7:14 says, *"If my people which are called by my name, shall humble themselves, and pray, and seek my face, and turn from their wicked ways; then will I hear from heaven and will forgive their sins and will heal their land."* Note, God is saying if **MY** people do this, not those who don't know Him. We are called to be prayer-warriors and pray for those in authority so we can live peaceable lives.

Prayers of Declaration: In these prayers, we pray the Scriptures over ourselves or others. These are powerful prayers because we are praying God's words back to Him. And when we do, we know we are praying according to His will. We are partnering with God and saying what He says about us or our situation. For example, if we are fearful about doing something we can pray: *"I can do all things through Christ who strengthens me."* Or, *"Greater is he that is in me than he that is in the world,"* etcetera. In other words, we match Scripture with the need.

There are three steps here. First, locate God's promise in His Word regarding the thing needed. Then fulfill the condition/s attached to the promise. And third, by faith, claim the promise.

Prayer of Agreement: In Matthew 18:19, Jesus said, *"If two of you shall agree on earth as touching anything that they shall ask, it shall be done for them of my Father which is in heaven."* It's the prayer of unity. And unity is powerful. When the body of Christ is unified, it can move mountains. That's why Satan tries to sow disunity in churches. If he can divide, he can conquer. Husbands and wives can pray together for their children, making their prayers more powerful than if they prayed separately. Members of a church can pray for their pastors and so on. The devil hates these prayers.

Prayers of Binding and Loosing (Spiritual Warfare Prayers): These are power prayers and involve taking authority over Satan and his demons. Many in the church shy away from this because it makes them uncomfortable or even frightened. But we must remember it's not by our authority and power that we come against Satan. It's by God's power and authority. We **never** come against him in our own name, only in the name of Jesus. And we must be authorized to use that name by being a born-again believer, having accepted Jesus as our Lord and Savior.

Remember what happened to the seven sons of Sceva in Acts 19:14-15? They tried coming against an evil spirit, and yes, they even used the name of Jesus. But they couldn't fool the spirit. It said, *"Jesus I know, and Paul I know; but who are ye?"* Then all seven of them ended up getting stripped and beaten. They were not followers of Christ but had seen His works and thought they could do them simply by using His name. They found out the hard way it wasn't so.

But we, the body of Christ, not only have the power but the obligation to take authority over the works of the devil. This and other information relating to spiritual warfare will be covered in more detail in Chapter 9 entitled, **Is Satan real?**

In Matthew 12:28-29 Jesus said, *"But if I cast out devils by the Spirit of God, then the kingdom of God is come unto you. Or else how can one enter into a strong man's house, and spoil his goods, except he first bind the strong man? And then he will spoil his house."* That word bind is *deo* and means "to be in bonds, knit, tie." Here, Jesus is giving us a blueprint of spiritual warfare prayers. When we pray for ourselves or someone who is under demonic attack, we need to bind the evil spirit or spirits in the name of Jesus.

And Hebrews 1:13-14 says, *"But to which of the angels said he at any time, Sit on my right hand, until I make thine enemies thy footstool? Are they not all ministering spirits, sent forth to minister for them who shall be heirs of salvation?"* Yes, we have guardian angels. And since we are heirs of salvation, we can and should, after binding the enemy, lose our ministering angels into the situation. By doing so, we active them on our behalf.

It's all very simple. And there's nothing scary about it. Jesus never shouted at the demons or had lengthy conversations with them. He simply said, "get out, be gone," etcetera, and they were gone. This should be our example as well.

Prayers of Intercession: This usually follows a burden that comes upon a prayer's heart along with the willingness to stand in the gap for a specific person in prayer. Romans 15:1 tells us that we should *"bear the infirmities of the weak."* That word "infirmities" means "sickness" as well as "feeble strengthless, impotent, weak." In other words, it's a person who is incapable of fighting the battle himself and needs someone to stand in the gap. Aside from praying for an individual, prayers of intercession are also prayed for nations and groups of people. I Timothy 2:1-4 instructs us to pray for those in authority over us. And in Ephesians 1:15-23 Paul prayed for the church in Ephesus.

These prayers often require spiritual warfare because usually those for whom we are interceding are under attack, in some way, by the enemy of their soul, the devil. Because of this, it would be wise to first put on the whole armor of God. Then authority over Satan and his demonic forces must be taken, as well as forbidding them to interfere with or inject themselves into the prayer time. Then, as in other prayers, we enter God's courts with thanksgiving and praise. We should thank God for His wisdom, His knowledge and His revelation that He will be giving us through the power of the Holy Spirit so we can be effective prayer warriors.

Praying in tongues is invaluable here since many times we won't know what is going on in the person's life, the one for whom we are now interceding. Romans 8:26 says, *"Likewise the Spirit also helpeth our infirmities: for we know not what we should pray for as we ought: but the Spirit itself maketh intercession for us with groanings which cannot be uttered."* We admit to God that we really don't know how to pray and ask the Holy Spirit to pray through us.

Throughout this time, we should have our Bible and note pad nearby, and write down anything the Holy Spirit brings to mind. Then pray through whatever is on the pad, not stopping until we receive peace from God. Sometimes, God will give us nothing to write. In that case, just continue praying in tongues. This burden of intercession can last for hours or even days. We stop only when the burden is lifted.

This type of praying can be exhausting and should not be entered lightly. But be aware that these prayers can bring a wayward child back home, can break addictions over a person's life, save a marriage or heal the desperately ill. They are powerful and have far reaching consequences, even when no results are immediately evident.

Conclusion:

God is able. Ephesians 3:20 says, *"Now unto Him* (Jesus) *that is able to do exceeding abundantly above all that we ask or think, according to the power that worketh in us."* God can do anything. And He has given us power to activate His Word in our lives and in the lives of others. We should never underestimate the power of our prayers. James 5:16b says, *"The effectual fervent prayer of a righteous man availeth much."* If we are saved, then we are righteous and our prayers can accomplish much. Our prayers don't have to be eloquent and should not follow a formula but be respectful and sincere. They should come from the heart.

Hebrews 11:6b also tells us that, *"he* (God) *is a rewarder of them that diligently seek him."* So, we need to put God in first place, trust Him and be people of prayer, and then watch all the amazing things He will do!

Question Six: *How Can I be Sure God Loves Me?*

"I made a lot of mistakes before coming to the Lord. If I mess up again, will God still love me?"

We can take comfort in

Psalms 103:12 which says if we belong to the Lord and confess our sins then, *"As far as the east is from the west, so far hath he removed our transgressions from us."* Micah 7:19b goes on to say that God will, *"cast all their* (the believers') *sins into the depths of the sea."* And then there's this in Hebrews 8:12, *"For I will be merciful to their unrighteousness, and their sins and their iniquities will I remember no more."* Imagine that! If we confess our sins, God not only forgives them but chooses not to remember them anymore. He's never going to bring them up or throw them in our face. He's never going to say, "Remember when you lied? And what about the time you said those unkind things?" NO. God will never never never bring them up again.

Not only that, but Romans 8:1 clearly states our position in Christ. *"There is therefore now no condemnation to them which are in Christ Jesus, who walk not after the flesh, but after the Spirit."* So, if we have repented and put our sins under the blood of Jesus, we should not feel condemned. If we do, it's not from God. It's either coming from the enemy of our soul, the devil, or from our inability to forgive ourselves.

Romans 8:34-39 reaffirms this by saying that Christ does not condemn us. And nothing, absolutely nothing, can separate us from the love of God. We could stop right here and have everything we'd ever need to feel forgiven, accepted and loved by God.

After I had children and came to the Lord, I began to understand God's great love for me by how much I loved my children. God is our Father. We are His children. What parent doesn't want what's best for his child and doesn't do all to protect that child? What parent doesn't hurt when his child hurts? And what parent doesn't rejoice over the successes and happy moments in a child's life? Well, it's the same for God. He is the perfect parent. His heart breaks when ours breaks. He rejoices when we rejoice. And He wants only what's best for us.

And because God loves us so much, He cares about the things we care about. Even the little things. After I lost an earring, I asked God to help me find it. Yes, I asked God to bother about my earring. It was a pierced earring, thin gold and in the shape of a triangle. It was the first piece of jewelry my husband gave me after we were married, so it had great sentimental value. Several days after my request, I spotted it right outside my front door, just sitting there as if some hand had placed it, stem side up. I had come in and out of that door dozens of times since the loss, and never saw a thing. But suddenly, there it was!

A day or two later, I realized I only had metal or plastic backings—those tiny pieces that slide over the stem of the earring to secure it—but no gold to replace the one I lost. So, again I asked God to help me find it. I knew in my heart there was nothing He couldn't do. Sure enough, while I was vacuuming the living room rug, a little gold object suddenly popped up from the floor and flew into the air. You guessed it! It was the gold backing. That the God of the universe would spend one second recovering my earring and backing still blows my mind. But that's Who He is. That's the sweet, intimate, loving, caring God we serve!

Another time, when my husband and I were thinking of selling our first house, we decided to ask God to be our real estate agent. We felt we should do our part by putting a "house for sale" ad in the local paper which ran from Thursday through Sunday. It turned out that those were the very days a huge snowstorm hit the area. Our house was a basic high ranch. The highlights were the beautiful sunroom—with glass windows in the ceiling and along three walls—and four tiers of decking leading to an oval pool, all of which my husband built.

Only one couple braved the slick, snowy roads to view the house, and that was late Sunday afternoon. By then, the sunroom, pool and decks were covered by a thick blanket of snow. How were we to sell our house when no one could see its best features? *Oh, ye of little faith!* A few hours after the viewing, the couple called telling us they wanted the house. Within a week, we had a signed contract. Nothing, nothing, nothing is impossible with God. And nothing, nothing, nothing is too small or too big for Him to handle. He cared about my earring and our house because it was important to us. And He cares about everything that is important to you.

The Bible tells us God is Love. But what does that look like?

1 Corinthians 13:4-8 describes it well. *"Charity* (love) *suffereth long, and is kind; charity envieth not; charity vaunteth not itself, is not puffed up, Doth not behave itself unseemly, seeketh not her own, is not easily provoked, thinketh no evil; Rejoiceth not in iniquity, but rejoiceth in the truth; Beareth all things, believeth all things, hopeth all things, endureth all things. Charity never faileth."*

So, if God is love that means He is patient, kind, isn't envious, is humble, isn't touchy or resentful, not easily provoked, rejoices in truth and justice, is hopeful and longsuffering, and He never fails.

Wow!

Of course, Jesus is God's perfect example of love. John 3:16 says, *"For God so loved the world, that he gave his only begotten Son, that whosoever believed in him should not perish, but have everlasting life."*

Then, in John 14:7-9, Jesus said if you know Him you know the Father, and if you see Him you've seen the Father. In other words, they are one, their characters are one. To know Jesus is to know God the Father.

The gospels reveal that Jesus' most outstanding characteristic is compassion (love). In Matthew 9:35-36, we see Jesus teaching and preaching and healing **every** sickness and disease. And it goes on to say that He was, *"moved with compassion"* because they had no shepherd, no one to lead them on the right path to God.

Again, in Matthew 14:14 Jesus is, *"moved with compassion"* and heals the sick. In Matthew 20:34 Jesus has *compassion* on two blind men and heals them. In Mark 1:41 Jesus, *"moved with compassion,"* heals a leper. In Matthew 15:32 Jesus' *compassion* has Him feed the four thousand. *Compassion,* in Luke 7:13, moves Jesus to raise the widow's son from the dead. And on it goes.

Jesus' compassion, His love, was the kind that always showed itself in action. It wasn't just a feeling. Rather, His feelings required Him to do something. And He did it.

And oh, how His heart broke when He stood looking over Jerusalem as He visualized Israel's coming destruction because of their rejection of Him. It made Him weep, again revealing His tender heart of love. Matthew 23:37 and Luke 19:41 tell us that Jesus had wanted to gather Israel, *"as a hen gathereth her chickens under her wings and ye would not!"*

The truth is, God has always loved us. Romans 5:8 tells us that, *"God commended his love toward us, in that while we were yet sinners, Christ died for us."* Even when we didn't love Him or want anything to do with Him, God loved us. And because of that love, Jesus died, knowing that not everyone would accept what He did and be saved. It must break His heart to know He provided a remedy with the promise of eternal life and still there would be many who'd reject it.

Even in the Old Testament, God demonstrated His love in the way He dealt with Noah, giving him time to build the ark so that the entire human race wouldn't perish. And when He promised Abraham He wouldn't destroy Sodom if only ten righteous people could be found, He revealed His heart of mercy and forgiveness. And when ten weren't found, He made sure Lot and his wife and two daughters were safely removed before destruction fell. Then there's the story of how God delivered Israel from Egyptian bondage; how He feed them for forty years in the wilderness during which time not even their clothes and shoes wore out! (Deuteronomy 29:5) And throughout it all, God put up with their murmuring and complaining and still brought their offspring into the promised land.

Isaiah 63:9b tells us how God dealt with Israel. *"In his love and in his pity he redeemed them; and he bare them, and carried them all the days of old."*

Oh, the goodness of God! His love, mercy and longsuffering are evident to anyone who cares to see.

I believe understanding God's love is the cornerstone of a full Christian life. God loves us so much that He gave everything at the cross for us. Unfortunately, many Christians believe in Jesus' atoning work without grasping the depth of God's love for them.

Three reasons why it's important to know God loves us.

First: so, we can love Him back. It's hard to love someone we don't think loves us. If we think God is mad at us all the time or judging us all the time or that we are constantly disappointing Him, it will be difficult to love Him.

Second: so, we can love ourselves. Knowing how much our Creator values us will enable us to value ourselves. If we rely on the world or others to determine our value, we're going to be unhappy and disappointed.

Third: so, we can then love others. If we don't love ourselves it will be difficult to love anyone else. The expression "hurting people hurt others" is true. Those who are hurting and don't value themselves will generally be unable to value or love anyone else. Their pain will constantly make them look for validation anywhere they can get it, even at the expense of others.

Now, let's take a closer look at each of these three things.

First, Loving God:

Jesus, in Matthew 22:37, commandments, *"Thou shalt love the Lord thy God with all thy heart and with all thy soul and with all thy mind."*

Notice, it's a command. And being a command means it's doable. God would never command us to do something impossible, even if most of the time that means He must enable us to do it via His Holy Spirit.

But even with the Holy Spirit, loving God isn't always easy. Many earthly fathers have spoiled the concept of God the Father for their children due to their cruelty, neglect or indifference. This must be overcome through inner healing. It's going to take God touching that rejection, those hurts, betrayals, neglect to bring wholeness, and enable those hurting to trust Him as Father.

Along the way, our adversary, the devil, will do all he can to discourage us. One of Satan's best tactics is to convince us that God doesn't love us. After we come to the Lord, and the Holy Spirit begins working in us, we'll start clearly seeing more of our faults. That's when Satan will tell us, "God can't possibly love you!" And should we fall and sin, he'll be right there to point out our failure. He'll whisper things like, "How many times do you expect God to forgive this?" But 1 John 4:19 says, *"we love Him* (Jesus/God) *because he first loved us."* It's amazing, but God has always loved us, even way before we began loving Him.

It is absolutely essential to know that God loves us. And I'm not talking about head knowledge. I believe every Christian has some level of that. But we need more. We need heart knowledge.

We also need to remember that we never earned God's love by anything we did. So, we can't lose God's love by anything we do. The more we understand and believe in our heart that God truly loves us—as imperfect as we are—the more we can overcome Satan's lies. This, in turn, helps us to love and trust God more, have a closer walk with Him, allow Him to work in us and make us His vessel. When we love someone, we want to please that person. So, the more we love God, the more we'll want to please Him. And we do this by obeying His Word.

And oh, the benefits of loving God! Psalms 91:14 says, *"Because he* (meaning us) *hath set his love upon me* (God), *therefore will I deliver him: I will set him on high, because he hath known my name."* What a promise! If we love God, He promises that He will deliver us. And that word "high" is *sagab* in Hebrew and means, "inaccessible, strong, be safe, defend." So, God will deliver, defend and keep safe those who love Him.

Proverbs 8:17 says, *"I* (God) *love them that love me and those that seek me early shall find me."* God will never turn anyone away who wants to know, love or serve Him.

God's love still amazes me. So does the knowledge that He longs for our fellowship and our love. And the relationship He wants is not casual but intimate. That's why, in both the Old and New Testament, God uses the picture of a bride and bridegroom to illustrate the depth of the relationship He desires. Among the examples in the Old Testament is Song of Songs where this truth is illustrated in the love relationship between the king and the Shulamite woman. In the New Testament, it is illustrated in the relationship between Jesus and the Church, which He calls His "bride."

Psalms 22:9-10; 71:6; 139:13-14 indicate that God knows us completely. It says He knew us while we were still in our mother's womb. We are no accident, no mistake. We are wanted and loved by God and have a purpose. Matthew 10:30 tells us that the very hairs of our head are numbered. Also, God promises that He'll never leave us or forsake us. And in Jeremiah 31:3 God says, *"I have loved you with an everlasting love."*

Since God is love, since His very nature is love, He can't do anything but love us, even when our actions are unlovable. However, this doesn't negate God's command that we are to be holy as He is holy. And if we are not, if we persist in ungodly ways, He will, as a loving Father, discipline us.

But it's all worth it. I Corinthian 2:9 tells us that, *"Eye has not seen, nor ear heard, neither have entered into the heart of man, the things which God has prepared for them that love him."* We can't even imagine what wonders await us. Wonders God has prepared just for us!

Loving ourselves:

Everyone needs love. Without love, a soul withers. Unfortunately, many people don't feel loved. And often, this makes them look for love in all the wrong places. Some give themselves away sexually. Others try to find validation by amassing riches. Still others strive for titles, success or recognition in various areas. I'm not speaking about wanting to do our best, to do all as unto the Lord. I'm talking about titles, success or recognition for their own sake. In those cases, root and desire are the same: *If I do this or if I accomplish that—**then** someone will see my value and love me.*

A person who doesn't feel loved and who doesn't love himself cannot love others properly. There are many wounded Christians who don't love themselves, and in turn, wound others.

In John 11:44, after Jesus called Lazarus out of the tomb, it says *"and he* (Lazarus) *that was dead came forth, bound hand and foot with grave clothes; and his face was bound about with a napkin. Jesus saith unto them, Loose him, and let him go."* In the same way, when Jesus raised us from the dead and brought us into new life with him causing us to became "born again," we were still bound with grave clothes—those old rotten things still clinging to us from our former life, including wounds. We need to be loosed.

Life has dealt everyone blows; some more than others. But we all have sinned against others and ourselves (overeating, taking drugs, drunkenness, sex outside marriage, walking in fear rather than walking in God's Word, etc.). And others have sinned against us. All these require forgiveness; God's and ours.

So, the first step in loving ourselves is forgiveness. We need to ask God to forgive **us** for sinning against others and ourselves. We also need to forgive **others** for sinning against us. And we need to forgive **ourselves**. Without all this forgiveness, there will be NO healing, NO wholeness, NO loving of self. When we forgive someone, it doesn't mean we are saying what that person did was okay. It means we give up all right to harbor anger, resentment or revenge against that person. We let God deal with him.

The next step is renewing our mind. We need to see ourselves as God sees us. And that means getting into the Word. Just listening to a Sunday sermon isn't going to cut it. Hebrews 4:12 tells us that, *"the word of God is quick, and powerful, and sharper than any twoedged sword, piercing even to the dividing asunder of soul and spirit, and of the joints and marrow, and is a discerner of the thoughts and intents of the heart."* Among other things, it means that as we get into God's Word it will separate the false perception we have of ourselves from the real perception God has. We begin to see ourselves and others, as well as situations in our life, through God's eyes.

2 Timothy 1:7 tells us that, *"God has not given us a spirit of fear, but of power, and of love, and of a sound mind."* While 1 Corinthians 2:16 tells us, we have the mind of Christ. So, we need to start operating in it. Proverbs 3:7-8 says, *"Be not wise in thine own eyes: fear the LORD, and depart from evil. It shall be health to thy navel, and marrow to thy bones."* We are to depart from the old way of thinking, from our evil, negative thoughts and ways of doing things, and meditate on God's Word. That is our road to health and healing.

Proverbs 4:20-22 says, *"My son, attend to my words;* (Solomon is really talking about God's wisdom here) *incline thy ear unto my sayings. Let them not depart from thine eyes; keep them in the midst of thine heart. For they are life unto those that find them, and health to all their flesh."* Again, don't miss it. God's Word is life and health. When we study the Word, we begin to **learn** what God thinks about us. But that's only part of it. We also need to **speak** these words over ourselves. Proverbs 12:18b says, *"the tongue of the wise is* (brings) *health."* So, the words of life we speak will bring health to our wounded souls.

But it doesn't end there. We are not only to speak the Word but **live** it. When we do, we'll find ourselves in harmony with God, filled with His peace and joy.

Even after all this, we may need deliverance. Curses may need to be broken over our lives, spirits of inheritance rebuked, family sins confessed. Did you know that spirits of poverty and bondage (to alcohol, etc.), just to name two, can follow a family bloodline for generations? And these are all hindrances to loving ourselves.

I've already mentioned the importance of inner healing. The truth is, I believe everyone needs this. If you've lived long enough in this broken world, chances are, at some point, you've been hurt, disappointed, misunderstood, taken advantage of, etcetera. Early on in my walk with the Lord, He showed me that because I was adopted, I carried a deep-seated feeling of rejection. And if I didn't let Him deal with it, it could affect every relationship in my life. Honestly, I didn't even know I had that problem, which goes to show you how little we really know ourselves. But I was obedient and allowed God to touch that deep place in my heart. Since then, I've come to see how important and necessary that inner healing was. It's all part of getting rid of those grave clothes.

You don't need to go to anyone for this, though going to the right person may be helpful. Let God direct you. But just know that this can be done between you and God. And if you do this alone with God, block out some time and sit quietly before Him. Have a notebook and pen handy. Then do spiritual warfare, binding any evil spirits from interfering in this time with the Lord. After that, allow the Lord to recall an incident or series of incidences that need His healing touch. Keep a journal. Take it slow. Allow the Holy Spirit complete charge. Don't be afraid to see a situation through God's eyes. But don't expect that after one session with God everything in your life has been healed. Rather, God, because He is so gentle, often approaches our wounds like an onion and peels off only one layer at a time. But as He does, we begin to value ourselves more and more. Remember: hurting people hurt people. God wants us whole, not only for ourselves but for the benefit of others.

Loving Others:

In John 15:12, Jesus commands us to, *"love one another as I have loved you."* So, not only are we to love God but we are to love each other. And what's more, we are to love each other like Jesus loves us. That's a tall order. But again, it's a command, so that means it's doable. But we can only do this after we've come to love ourselves.

Romans 5:5b says, *"the love of God is shed abroad in our hearts by the Holy Ghost which is given unto us."* That means we don't have to conjure it up or force it. Love is already there. And the more inner healing we experience, the fewer obstacles will prevent this love from spilling over onto others. Jesus said in John 13:35, *"By this shall all men know that ye are my disciples, if ye have love one to another."* So, love is the outward sign that we are His disciples.

Jesus said in John 15:9, *"As the Father hath loved me, so have I loved you: continue ye in my love."* Understand that Jesus expects us to walk in love, to live our lives loving others. He expects this because He has given us the means to do it.

Colossians 3:12-14 is a picture of a believer who loves God, himself and others: *"Put on therefore, as the elect of God, holy and beloved, bowels of mercies, kindness, humbleness of mind, meekness, longsuffering; Forbearing one another, and forgiving one another, if any man have a quarrel against any: even as Christ forgave you, so also do ye. And above all these things put on charity* (love)*, which is the bond of perfectness."*

And that is how God wants each of us to live and function. May it be so for us all in Jesus' wonderful name.

Question Seven: *Does God want us well?*

Yes.

God's perfect will is that everyone be healed and whole, and that means spiritually, emotionally and physically. This truth is reflected in Scripture. When Jesus received thirty-nine lashes, He took our sicknesses upon Himself. Isaiah 53:5 is talking about Jesus, the Messiah, and says, *"But he was wounded for our transgressions, he was bruised for our iniquities: the chastisement of our peace was upon him; and with his stripes we are healed."* Notice, it's already done. Jesus paid for our wholeness, our wellness. Did you know that if we are saved, if we are a born-again believer, that very word, "salvation" includes healing? But it must be appropriated by faith.

In addition, Jesus not only wants people well, but He gave believers the command, authority and power to heal the sick. Matthew 10:1 says, *"And when he* (Jesus) *had called unto him his twelve disciples, he gave them power against unclean spirits, to cast them out, and to heal all manner of sickness and all manner of disease."* Jesus also said in Mark 16:17-18, *"And these signs shall follow them that believe: in my name shall they cast out devils; they shall speak with new tongues; They shall take up serpents; and if they drink any deadly thing, it shall not hurt them;* ***they shall lay hands on the sick, and they shall recover****."* Jesus expects believers to not only be healthy and well themselves, but to heal others.

It's the devil who comes to steal, kill and destroy. It's Jesus who come to give us abundant life. (John 10:10)

Jesus' entire ministry is an example. He never refused to heal anyone. In fact, Matthew 4:23 says, *"And Jesus went about all Galilee, teaching in their synagogues, and preaching the gospel of the kingdom, and healing* ***all*** *manner of sickness and* ***all*** *manner of disease among the people."* Notice the word "all." Matthew 9:35 reiterates this by saying Jesus went about teaching and preaching and healing, *"****every*** *sickness and* ***every*** *disease among the people."*

Then, consider the Lord's Prayer. This is the prayer Jesus taught His disciples. In it is this: *"Thy* (God's) *will be done in earth, as it is in heaven."* There is no sickness in heaven. Therefore, one must conclude that God desires there be no sickness on earth, either.

Even in the Old Testament, God equated health with Divine favor. In Exodus 23:25b, God promises Israel if they served Him, then He would, *"take sickness away from the midst of thee."* Deuteronomy 7:15 restates this. God, through Moses, promises the Israelites that if they remain faithful to Him, then He the *"LORD will take way from thee all sickness."*

So, why are people sick?

First off, we live in a fallen world full of disease producing organisms. In addition, our produce is sprayed with poisons. Our meat is injected with growth hormones and antibiotics. Our packaged food is full of chemicals and compounds we can't even pronounce. Our water is often contaminated with bacteria, chemicals and pharmaceutical drugs. Most of our hair, skin, and body products are loaded with harmful additives. Much of our furniture, rugs as well as household cleaners emit harmful vapors.

Any one of these can make a person sick. It's not God's fault that we have polluted practically everything we've touched, and therefore inhale, ingest and absorb destructive toxins every day. It's only because man is so *"fearfully and wonderfully made"* by God (Psalms 139:14) that anyone manages to maintain their health.

Another reason is because we are fallen ourselves and can pass predispositions to diseases to our offspring, as well as weakened immune systems, weakened organs, etcetera.

Our very lifestyle can also contribute to this scenario. If we eat a dozen donuts in the morning and down a pint of Scotch at night, how surprised should we be if we end up with diabetes or cirrhosis of the liver? The answer is, not very. And it would hardly be fair to blame God for our excesses.

Another cause of declining health and sickness is the overuse of medicines and drugs. God can and does use doctors to help restore health. And I certainly don't advise anyone to leave their doctor or discontinue their meds. But the fact remains that nowadays there are pills for everything, and people are too eager to take them. We must understand that **every** medication, including those non-prescription over-the-counter meds, have side effects. Every one! And what can happen is that the pill someone takes may help his current issue, only to produce additional issues, which then require more medication, which in turn produce more side effects. It can become a vicious cycle.

Stress is also a critical factor. Scientists have proven that not only stress but worry, anxiety and fear can make people sick. And the world is a very stressful place and becoming more so. It can give us much to be anxious and fearful about if we let it. But, to the above list I'd add, unforgiveness (carrying grudges, hatred, anger) and deliberately sinning—all health and healing blockers.

Then, there's the enemy of our soul, the devil. Can he make people sick? Yes, if we open ourselves up to him. When I was associated with Women's Aglow, we had a guest speaker who said for twenty-five years she was constantly sick. Like the woman with the issue of blood, she had seen numerous doctors, none of whom could help. After she came to the Lord, He showed her what had happened. Twenty-five years prior, she, her husband, and some friends had gone to a nightclub where the featured entertainer was a hypnotist. He had called for a volunteer to prove his abilities, and when no one came forward, he coerced this woman to oblige him. He successfully put her under, had her bark like a dog, hop on one leg, flap like a chicken, then woke her up. God showed her that when someone is under hypnosis, it opens that person up to the demonic realm. That's how the spirit of infirmity got a foothold and sickened her all those years.

To some, this may sound farfetched but ask anyone who has been caught up in the occult or found himself under the influence of an evil spirit and he will tell you the horror and truth of it. There are spiritual realities that transcend the physical, and this is one of them. Dabbling in the occult is a sin and opens one up to demonic activity. What someone may believe is innocent fun can lead to a damaged and unhappy life.

After this woman came to the Lord, she confessed her sin, even though it was done in ignorance, then commanded the spirit to leave her, and she was free. Several years had passed from that time to her presentation at the Aglow meeting, during which she enjoyed perfect health. Praise God! He is Lord over every sickness and every demonic spirit!

Considering all the above, can we still walk in health?

Yes, but it will require effort on our part. I think the first step should be to do everything, physically, we can (exercise, eating healthy, etcetera) then concentrate on the spiritual. Among other things, this will require watching our words.

But that doesn't sound very spiritual. Perhaps not, but our words are powerful. Proverbs 18:21 tells us that, *"Death and life are in the power of the tongue: and they that love it shall eat the fruit thereof."* Our words are not only powerful, but creative, and actually produce fruit. And this is the fruit we will end up eating. Yes, we eat our words.

I had a friend who said that every December she always got sick. And guess what? Every December she got sick. She constantly spoke these negative words over herself, then had to eat the fruit they produced. What she was doing was cursing herself and giving Satan permission to make her sick each December. And he was happy to oblige.

Proverbs 18:7 should give us pause. *"A fool's mouth is his destruction, and his lips are the snare of his soul."* And Proverbs 21:23 cautions us by saying, *"Whoso keepeth his mouth and his tongue keepeth his soul from troubles."*

We are not to speak as fools. Our mouths should not be full of self-cursing but full of life. And the way we speak life is to speak God's Word over ourselves and others.

Proverbs 4:22 tells us that God's Word is health to our flesh. And Proverbs 12:18 says, *"the tongue of the wise is health."* When we speak God's Word over ourselves, we are calling those things which are not, into being (Romans 4:17) and partnering with God. His Word is supernatural and can heal us, even those who are desperately ill. I've heard testimonies of stage-4 cancers healed, tumors healed, hearing and sight healed, and so much more.

Psalm107:20 says that God, *"sent His Word and healed them."* That's what we're doing when we pray and confess Scripture. We are sending God's Word into that situation.

Two misconceptions about sickness and healing:

There are others, but the following are the ones I hear most often.

I can't tell you how many times I've caught people saying, "We all have a cross to bear. I guess this sickness, this disease is mine." They are calling their sickness their "cross" because they believe Luke 9:23 implies this. *"And he* (Jesus) *said to them all, If any man will come after me, let him deny himself, and take up his cross daily, and follow me."* (also see Matthew 16:24, Mark 8:34 and Luke 14:27)

Not one of these passages suggest we are to carry a load of burdens or various sicknesses. NO. Not at all. The cross is an instrument of death, and when we daily take up ours, it means we are daily dying to self so that there is more room for Christ. That way, we, like Paul, can say, *"I am **crucified** with*

Christ: nevertheless I live; Yet not I, but Christ liveth in me: and the life which I now live in the flesh I live by the faith of the Son of God, who loved me, and gave himself for me." (Galatians 2:20)

Paul was someone who took up his cross daily. After he came to the Lord, his life was spent obeying God even though it cost him. Yes, even after mobs stoned him, flogged him, chased him out of town. Even after he was imprisoned, shipwrecked and bitten by a poisonous snake. Even after all that, Paul was still willing to continue obeying the Lord. He had died to self and was now living only for God.

We must be willing to do the same. And that is only possible if we die to self, to our self-interest, selfishness, self-centeredness, etcetera and live, instead, for Jesus.

The next misconception is that God makes us sick in order to teach us something. This is so wrong on many levels. As already mentioned, if we are a believer, Jesus paid, not only for all our sins (by His blood) but for all our sickness (by His stripes, His thirty-nine lashes; remember that word "salvation" includes health and healing.) And think about it. What kind of parent would deliberately make their children sick in order to teach them something? The concept is absurd.

People who believe God made them sick, in order to teach them something, often cite the Scripture regarding Paul's thorn in the side. They say something like this, "Well, God didn't heal Paul's thorn, so I guess He's not going to heal mine." Or they say, "If God didn't heal Paul's thorn, and **he** wrote so much of the New Testament, why should He heal mine?"

Let's look at the Scripture they are referencing. 2 Corinthians 7-9, *"And lest I should be exalted above measure through the abundance of the revelations* (Paul was taken to heaven and heard 'unspeakable words') *there was given to me a thorn in the flesh, the messenger of Satan to buffet me, lest I should be exalted above measure. For this thing I besought the Lord, thrice, that it might depart from me. And he* (God) *said unto me, My grace is sufficient for thee: for my strength is made perfect in weakness."*

Let's unpack it. First, that word "thorn" is *skolops* in Greek and means "prickle, annoyance, disability, point." Next, that word flesh (*sarx*) means "the body, human nature, passions." Messenger (*aggelos*) means "messenger, angel." Buffet (*kolaphizo*) means "to rap, to curtail, chastise, punish."

What does all this tell us? It tells us that Paul had an incredible experience in heaven and in order to keep him humble, God allowed a fallen angel, Satan's messenger, to prick, annoy or try to put some disability on him. Notice, this "thorn" comes from Satan not God. And why did God allow Satan to annoy or harass or "buffet" Paul? So Paul wouldn't get too big for his buttons and begin thinking he was really something. So Paul would remember he needed God and needed to rely on Him instead of relying on himself. So Paul would appropriate God's grace.

But God didn't just leave it at that. Instead, He gave Paul the remedy. He didn't expect Paul to continue suffering. Rather, God expected Paul to rely on His grace to overcome the situation.

And what was Satan doing to Paul, anyway? It's not entirely clear. He may have been trying to make Paul ill. But Satan could just as easily have been harassing him in other ways, such as annoying him or pricking Paul's human nature and passions by providing situations that aroused his anger, frustration, fear, sadness, annoyance and the like. But whatever it was, the bottom line is still this, God's grace was more than able to handle it. His grace was the way out.

Ok, God wants us healed. But how do we get this healing for ourselves?

Supernatural healing is received by faith, by believing God's Word and speaking it over ourselves. I strongly advise anyone who needs healing to study and meditate on the healing Scriptures in order to appropriate them. I also highly recommend Becky Dvorak's book, *The Healing Creed*. It's an excellent scripturally-sound study on why we should believe healing belongs to us.

We need to get this right because there's plenty of faulty thinking regarding healing, including the ones mentioned above. Nowhere in the Bible can you find Jesus refusing to heal anyone! It's already been noted that Jesus paid a tremendous price for our healing. Thirty-nine lashes split open His back, lashes by a whip with three leather thongs, each weighted by pieces of metal or bone. It cost Him so much that it would be an **insult** to allow His sacrifice to go to waste by claiming it's a lesson from Him and refusing to appropriate our healing.

But if we do get sick, can He use it to teach us patience, compassion, longsuffering, etcetera? Of course, He can. God never wastes anything. He can and does use all the situations in our life, both good and bad, to bring us closer to Him and change us from glory to glory. But that doesn't mean He wants us sick.

Just look at a few Scriptures: I Corinthians 6:19, *"Know ye not that your body is the temple of the Holy Ghost which is in you?"* Matthew 8:17 says that Jesus Himself, *"took our infirmities, and bare our sicknesses."* 1 Peter 2:24, *"Who his own self bare our sins in his own body on the tree, that we, being dead to sins, should live unto righteousness: by whose stripes ye were healed."* Psalms 91:10, *"There shall no evil befall thee, neither shall any plague come nigh thy dwelling."*

Our bodies are God's temples. He wants to keep them healthy, whole, and pure. And since Jesus bore our sicknesses, we don't have to. Health and healing are already ours because of what Jesus accomplished. It's past tense! Not only that, but God even promises to keep plagues (sicknesses) from coming near us. Our job is to believe it.

Sometimes we'll need to have others pray for us in order to receive our healing. When I got shingles the first time, I did everything naturally and spiritually I could think of in order to get well. But the disease persisted for months, with no decrease in intensity or pain. Finally, I remembered James 5:14 which says, *"Is any sick among you? Let him call for the elders of the church; and let them pray over him, anointing him with oil in the name of the Lord."* So, that's what I did. I made an appointment and had my pastor, the assistant pastor and church secretary pray over me and anoint me with oil. Within two days I noticed a difference! The pain decreased. The sores began to heal. You can't go wrong following the Word of God. A few years later, I got shingles again. This time I didn't wait. I immediately asked for prayer and was anointed with oil. Within days, all symptoms decreased, and I began feeling better. And the shingles were of such short duration, it truly amazed me!

But if we don't get our healing, we must not feel condemned. Rather, we should remember God's great love for us and ask Him to show us if there's anything hindering the healing. If He shows us something, then we need to act on it. If He doesn't, then we must understand that God is sovereign. His timing is not our timing. His ways not our ways. Only God knows our hearts, our situations, and how they fit in with His plan and purposes. But His perfect will for us always remains that we be healthy and whole. Perhaps some will only experience it in a heavenly eternity where there is no sickness.

Question Eight: *Do Christians have to tithe?*

First, let's define "tithe." It means a tenth, and when applied to Biblical times, it included produce and livestock, as well as money. In fact, during Moses' time, the tithing of livestock and produce was mandatory. Under the Priestly Code, the tithe was given to the Levites for their Temple service. And out of their tithe, they were required to tithe a tenth to the priests. Since the Levites did not own land, this was the way God provided for them (Numbers 18:20-23). Every third year it changed. The tithe was used for the needs of the Levites as well as for widows, orphans and strangers.

Some scholars have debated whether there could have been up to three tithes, but modern consensus is that there was only one. The confusion lies in that the tithe was used in different ways during different times, such as the third and sixth years.

Tithing became so important that in Malachi (3:8-12), the last book of the Old Testament, God said, *"Will a man rob God? Yet ye have robbed me. But ye say,*

Wherein have we robbed thee? In tithes and offerings. Ye are cursed with a curse: for ye have robbed me, even this whole nation. Bring ye all the tithes into the storehouse, that there may be meat in mine house, and prove me now herewith, saith the LORD of hosts, if I will not open you the windows of heaven, and pour you out a blessing, that there shall not be room enough to receive it. And I will rebuke the devourer for your sakes, and He shall not destroy the fruits of your ground; neither shall your vine cast her fruit before the time in the field, saith the LORD of hosts. And all nations shall call you blessed: for ye shall be a delightsome land, saith the LORD of hosts."

We see here that God considered an unpaid tithe, robbery, and it came with a curse. We also see that blessings were attached to the tithe.

But that's Old Testament.

Did the early church teach tithing?

No, not for the first few hundred years. In fact, freedom in giving was emphasized. But as tithing caught on it came to mean one tenth of a person's increase, and that usually meant money.

Unfortunately, in modern times, the teaching of tithing has been misused and abused. Because of this, it has given non-believers a bad taste in their mouths and in some cases has become a stumbling block, preventing them from coming to Christ. Non-believers, when speaking of TV evangelists, often say, "All they want is your money."

How did we get to this point? By too many TV personalities, as well as pastors, using cohesion, bribery, guilt, and fear to generate funds. They say, "If you give me a thousand dollars (or some other sum) within 24 hours, then God will bless you and that thing you have been asking Him, will be granted." Of course, there are variations on this plea, but it all comes out meaning the same, "give money to me, my church, my ministry now and you'll be blessed. Don't give and you'll miss your blessing."

These are pressure tactics, much like the tactics of a used-car salesman. It makes the giver think he is about to get the best deal of his life but makes him fearful, too, because if he doesn't act right away, he'll lose out on the wonderful offer. It's also presumptuous because it makes the giver think he can force the hand of God on his behalf. In many ways, it has become an embarrassment to the church.

This kind of giving doesn't promote a genuine desire to give out of love for God or because it pleases Him. Rather, it's self-serving.

Okay, so what should a Christian do about giving?

The Bible tells us that every good and perfect gift is from above (James 1:17) and that God gives us the ability to get wealth (Deuteronomy 8:18). So, if everything is God's and every good thing comes from Him, and He gives us the talents and abilities to earn a living and prosper, shouldn't we return some of it for His use in supporting our church, different ministries, the poor, etcetera?

Of course.

In addition, Jesus, in Luke 6:38, connected giving to a spiritual law. "***Give, and it shall be given unto you;*** *good measure, pressed down, and shaken together, and running over, shall men give into your bosom.* ***For with the same measure that ye mete*** **(give)** ***withal it shall be measured to you again.***" And 2 Corinthians 9:6-7 says, "*He which soweth sparingly shall reap also sparingly; and he which soweth bountifully shall reap also bountifully. Every man according as he purposeth in his heart, so let him give; not grudgingly, or of necessity: for God loveth a cheerful giver. And God is able to make all grace abound toward you; that ye, always having all* *sufficiency in all things, may abound in every good work."*

What's described above is the Law of Reciprocity. Reciprocity means mutual action, a mutual exchange. That's what Jesus meant in Luke 6:38 when He said, *"Give and it will be given unto you."* He also said in Luke 6:31 that we were to do unto others as we would have them do unto us. In other words, action begets like action. The Law of Reciprocity says that violence begets violence, while kindness and love beget kindness and love. And giving (of yourself, your time, your money) begets giving. In other words, we will reap what we sow. But as mentioned in 2 Corinthians 9:6, if we sow sparingly, we will reap sparingly. And that applies to every aspect of our lives.

God owns the cattle on a thousand hills (Psalms 50:10). And Psalms 24:1 says, *"The earth is the Lord's and the fullness thereof."* Everything belongs to the Lord. And He wants to give it to us.

The thing is, God cannot give us the things He'd like unless we operate in His spiritual laws, and that includes the Law of Reciprocity. And when we don't, we can block His blessings. But giving enables Him to act on our behalf. That blessing may not be in monetary form. Instead, it could involve peace, joy, health, wisdom, etcetera.

And we bless God's heart when we give cheerfully. Why? Because it shows Him where our heart is. Matthew 6:21 says, *"For where your treasure is, there will your heart be also."* When we give God our treasure, our money, it shows our heart is centered on Him!

Conclusion:

New Testament believers are under grace and not the law. Because of this, we are not required to tithe, to give a tenth of our income. Rather, the amount is left up to us. But the Law of Reciprocity indicates giving is an essential Kingdom principle. If we give with the proper heart attitude, it pleases God and reaps rewards.

Personally, I like guidelines. So, for me, I value those set up in the Old Testament about giving a tenth with offerings on top of that. But I also like that as a New Testament believer, I'm free to give according to my conscience. I've seen people in church hold up empty envelopes during the offering because they were too embarrassed or ashamed to reveal they had nothing to give. This should never be. We have so much freedom in this area and no one should ever be looked down upon for their giving or lack of it. Let the Holy Spirit instruct us in this matter and allow Him to instruct others without making them feel shame or pressure.

Having said that, I believe because Jesus gave us everything, holding nothing back, we should not hold back, either. Christians should be happy and willing to support their church as well as other worthy ministries. God's work requires financing, and if the body of Christ doesn't do it, who will? Because we love God, we should want to further His kingdom and that requires both our time and money. But what one gives is a matter of the heart. And that's were God looks. In that respect, I'd prefer the church taught the Law of Reciprocity rather than tithing.

In Malachi 3:10 God says to **prove** Him with our tithes and offerings, our giving. It's the only place in Scripture that I'm aware of, that gives us permission to test God. I know it's Old Testament, but I believe the principle here also applies to New Testament giving. Therefore, I'm not surprised to hear of the many miracles God has done for those who have given. He honors His word, and that includes His spiritual laws. And when He says, *"give and it shall be given,"* He means it.

So, what is the appropriate manner in which a New Testament believer should give? He should give out of love for God and a willingness to further God's kingdom. He should give cheerfully and generously, allowing the Holy Spirit to guide him. And he should give, confidently, knowing that God sees both his heart and his gift. And in due season, he will reap the rewards.

And what is the appropriate manner in which pastors, ministers, evangelists and the like should obtain financial support? They should state their need and trust God to move on the hearts of the givers. Period.

Question Nine: *Is Satan real?*

Yes, make no mistake, Satan is real.

And he is our enemy. Ephesians 6:12 tells us that, *"we wrestle not against flesh and blood, but against principalities, against powers, against the rulers of darkness of this world, against spiritual wickedness in high places."* Ephesians also tells us to, *"Put on the whole armor of God, that you may be able to stand against the wiles of the devil."* And 1 Peter 5:8 reminds us to, *"be sober, be vigilant; because your adversary the devil, as a roaring lion, walketh about, seeking whom he may devour."*

It's obvious Satan is after us, and sooner or later we'll have to confront him. *Do we really? Can't we just focus on Jesus?*

Our focus should always be on Jesus and not on Satan. But that doesn't mean we put our head in the sand and pretend he doesn't exist. If we think ignoring him will make him go away, we are mistaken. If Jesus was tempted by Satan, what makes us think we won't be? Satan **will** come. And he'll come as a roaring lion, fierce and without pity, looking to devour us or our loved ones. We need to be ready.

Satan was the original sinner. Isaiah 14:12-14 lists his five "I wills" and details how this created being had the audacity to think he could usurp God, the Creator of all. In the end, the best he can do is counterfeit the things of God by setting up an illegitimate kingdom.

God created man because He desired fellowship with him and wanted a family. But after Adam sinned, Satan saw an opportunity to build his own family. Isaiah 14:12 says, *"How art thou fallen from heaven, O Lucifer, son of the morning."*

Lucifer is *heylel* in Hebrew and means "morning star." It also means "clear, shine, to make show, to boast, rave, foolish." And that word "son" in Hebrew is *ben* and means "builder of a family, to build."

At one time, Lucifer was beautiful, brilliant and high ranking. But something he did made him appear boastful and foolish and fall from his exalted position. We know it's when he rebelled against God and took one-third of the angels with him. As a fallen angel and "son of the morning" Satan is now busy building his family.

Contrast this with Jesus.

Jesus, in Revelation 22:16b, said of Himself, *"I am the root and offspring of David, and the bright and morning star."* Here, that word "morning star" in Greek means "superior, prior, dawn, daybreak, in front of," a very different word from the Hebrew word used to describe Satan as the morning star.

Isaiah 14:13-14 further exposes Satan's game plan.

*"For thou (*Lucifer*) has said in thine heart, I will ascend into heaven, I will exalt my throne above the stars of God: I will sit also upon the mount of the congregation in the sides of the north: I will ascend above the heights of the clouds; I will be like the most High."*

Here, we see Satan declaring his intention to elevate himself above God and sit, *"upon the mount of the congregation in the sides of the north."* What does that mean? A concordance tells us that "mount" means "mountain, to loam up," while congregation means "fixed time, an appointment."

For a fixed time, and Satan knows it's just a fixed time, Satan will be the god of this world. He will rise up or be elevated. But how exactly? That word "sides" means "flank, to be soft, the *thigh.*" And that word "north" means "hidden, to hide, lurk, gloomy and unknown." Satan is going to use this fixed time to counterfeit the things of God and build his own family, and he's going to do it hidden and unknown in the thigh of man. Because man fell, Satan can do this.

But the thigh? That sounds strange. Or is it? Let's look at what the Bible says about the thigh. First, that word means "to be soft," which indicates it's vulnerable. But it also symbolizes power. A sword is worn on the thigh (Psalm 45:3, Song of Solomon 3:8). So, while the thigh denotes power, it's also vulnerable.

In addition, it signifies the generative parts, reproduction, offspring or fruit of the body. Samson, in Judges 15:8, smote the Philistines, *"hip and thigh with a great slaughter."* What was he doing? He was exacting judgment on that nation by cutting off future generations, both their seed and their potential accomplishments.

The strongest oaths involved the thigh. Both Abraham and Israel (Jacob) made others swear to them by having those people place their hand under their thigh (Genesis 24:2, Genesis 47:29).

And Revelation 19:16 says, *"And he* (Jesus) *hath on his vesture and on his* ***thigh*** *a name written, King of Kings, and Lord of Lords."*

Putting it all together, we see that Satan plans, without us knowing, to build his family by controlling man and affecting his fruits, which involves not only man's accomplishments but his offspring. And he'll do it by exploiting man's vulnerabilities.

If a person, no matter how nice he is, is not part of the family of God, he is part of the family of Satan. Harsh? Sometimes the truth is harsh. It's more appealing to hear, "we are all children of God" or "God loves us." Yes, God does love us, and yes, He wants everyone to be His child but sadly not everyone is or wants to be.

That's why 1 John 3:7-10a says, *"Little children let no man deceive you: he that doeth righteousness is righteous, even as he* (Jesus) *is righteous. He that committeth sin is of the devil; for the devil sinneth from the beginning . . . Whosoever is born of God* (being spiritually born-again) *doth not commit sin; for his* (God's) *seed remaineth in him; and he cannot sin, because he is born of God. In this the* ***children*** *of God are manifest and the* ***children*** *of the devil."* Here we see the two families.

Both families—the family of God and the family of Satan—were represented before the judgement seat of Pilate.

Jesus called God his Abba, His Father or Daddy. He was the Son of Abba, the Son of God. Barabbas was also the son of abba. Bar means son, abbas means belonging to father. Put it together and Barabbas means son of abba. But he wasn't God's son. He was Satan's. And Barabbas, like his father, was a thief, a liar and a murderer.

And just as the crowd chose Barabbas over Jesus, so the crowd, the world, still prefers the wrong son of abba. In John 15:18, Jesus said, *"If the world hates you, ye know that it hated me before it hated you."* The world will always love its own. It will never love us because we, believers, are not of this world.

Now, let's look at Jacob. Originally, he was not a committed believer. You could say he initially belonged to the family of Satan even though he came from Abraham and Isaac. Remember, Esau also came from that blood line and he certainly wasn't a man of God. We are not born into the family of God, physically. We must be born into it, spiritually. For Jacob, this spiritual rebirth was a long time in coming.

Here's how it happened.

In Genesis 32:24, after a falling out and years of separation, Jacob is preparing to face his brother, Esau. He fears Esau is still carrying a grudge over being tricked out of his birthright and blessing. Would he kill Jacob and his family? Not wanting to take that chance, Jacob separates his wives, children, possessions and servants into three groups. Hopefully, this way some of them might survive. And after he formed the groups, Genesis says, *"Jacob was left alone."*

Our decision to come to God must always be made by us. No one can do it for us. In that, we are alone. While he was alone, Jacob wrestled with God. This is when Jacob makes the transition. This is when he comes into the family of God.

Prior to this, in Genesis 28, when Jacob dreams of a ladder reaching heaven then receives God's promise to protect him and be with him and give him a land grant, Jacob acknowledges he encountered God. But he says this in Genesis 28:20-21, *"**If** God will be with me, and will keep me in this way that I go, and will give me bread to eat, and raiment to put on, So that I come again to my father's house in peace; **then** shall the LORD be my God."* He's not making a true commit to God, here. Rather, it's futuristic and almost cynical, one that hinges on God's performance.

Now, years later (Genesis 32:24-29) Jacob and God (pre-incarnate Jesus) wrestle. God has indeed protected Jacob, prospered him, given him bread and raiment and was sending him back to his father's house, though peace was not assured. Still, it was time for Jacob to honor the words he spoke in Genesis 28 and get serious with God. And while wrestling, God touches Jacob's *thigh*, the seat of his power and future achievement and fruit. And God changed Jacob's name to Israel. That name "Jacob" meant supplanter while "Israel" means prince with God.

Jacob limped because of God's touch, changing forever the way he walked through life. This indicates a price must be paid. Jacob had to give up his power and surrender to God. Once we surrender to God, the way we walk will change, too. We will no longer walk like the people of the world. And *only* after we have come into the family of God can we do spiritual battle with Satan.

James 4:7 says, *"Submit yourselves therefore to God. Resist the devil, and he will flee from you."* Submission to God must come before the fleeing of the devil.

Knowing the enemy means knowing his tactics and characteristics.

In Matthew 12:24, Satan is called, *"prince of the devils,"* and Ephesian 2:2 calls him the, *"prince of the power of the air."* Satan is a supernatural being who rules a host of fallen angels and an evil kingdom of supernatural spirits.

John 10:10 tells us that Satan comes as a thief, *"to steal, to kill and to destroy."* He will steal, kill and destroy everything he can in our lives. On the other hand, Jesus came, *"that they might have life, and that they might have it more abundantly."* What a contrast!

In John 8:44, Jesus calls Satan, *"a murderer from the beginning . . .* (and a*) liar and the father of it."*

And finally, Revelation 12:10 calls Satan, *"the accuser of our brethren."* Why? Because he will try to bring up every offense we have ever committed as well as all our failures.

From these Scriptures, we can know and understand how Satan operates. As a ruler over other demonic beings he has a vast army of dangerous minions at his disposal. His mission is to destroy whatever he can in our lives. But the ultimate goal is to destroy us by seeing we go to hell with him. As a liar, he twists and perverts the truth. And he will take every opportunity to remind us of our sins and failures.

In addition, 2 Corinthians 11:14 tells us, *"Satan himself is transformed into an angel of light."* That means he can come disguised as something good, something desirable. He is behind all false religions and cults. He has even invaded some Christian churches with perverted doctrines such as the anti-Sematic teaching of replacement theology and Chrislam, the blending of Islam and Christianity.

That is why we must know the Word of God.

Especially in these last days when the Bible says that many will be deceived and fall away. If we don't know Scripture, we will be open to any *"wind of doctrine."* (Ephesians 4:14) The kind of doctrine that sounds good, is inclusive, watered down and offends no one.

2 Corinthians 4:3-4 tells us, *"if our gospel be hid, it is hid to them that are lost. In whom the god of this world* (Satan) *hath blinded the* ***minds*** *of them which believe not, lest the light of the glorious gospel of Christ who is the image of God, should shine in them."*

Satan doesn't want anyone learning God's Word and will go to great lengths to prevent it. Look how the Word of God is forbidden in many countries! And look how the world tries to make those who believe in the Word seem foolish, uneducated, and dangerous. Satan blinds the minds of non-believers, his family. That's why people need to be prayed into the kingdom of God so that these spiritual blinders will be removed and then when they hear the gospel, God's word can penetrate.

Let's look at Satan in action.

In Genesis 3:1-6 Satan lies to Eve telling her that she could be like God if she eats the forbidden fruit. Then Eve misrepresents God's Word by saying He commanded her and Adam not to eat of that tree and *"neither shall ye touch it."* God never told her she couldn't touch it, just that she couldn't eat of it. Adding to or misrepresenting God's Word weakens it and can cause confusion. But that's one of Satan's best tactics, misrepresenting the Word of God.

Next, Satan used pride as the hook. After all, eating the forbidden fruit would make Eve like God! Pride then led to disobedience. Not surprising since the first sin ever committed was Satan's sin of pride (the 5 I wills) which in turn also led to disobedience.

Disobedience is always the natural outcome of pride because pride will make someone believe he knows better than God. In fact, most sin is rooted in pride. We get angry because we think, how could they do this to me! We hold grudges and are unforgiving because someone offended us. We improperly crave an abundance of material possessions in order to impress our neighbors. We often seek fame and power for the same reason. And on it goes.

Fear is another one of Satan's tools. 2 Timothy 1:7 says, *"For God hath not given us the spirit of fear; but of power, and of love and of a sound mind."* God actually commands us not to fear. And when we become fearful, it shows a lack of trust in Him.

The only proper fear is fear of God. Both 1 Peter 2:17 and Revelation 14:7 tells us to *"fear God."* And that word "fear" means "be in awe, revere, reverence." It means, as believers, we show God respect, reverence and honor because of Who He is. But there is another fear of God, a cringing fear that will be experienced by people who have rejected Him and who will endure His coming wrath.

How do we defeat Satan?

Remember James 4:7? *"Submit yourselves to God, resist the devil and he will flee."* We first come into the family of God, spiritually. We are "born-again." And once in the family, we need to continue to be submitted and obedient to God.

Second, we must realize that Satan is already defeated. In John 12:31 Jesus said, *"Now is the judgment of this world; now shall the prince of this world be cast out."* Jesus was speaking of His coming death. Through His death and resurrection almost 2000 years ago, He defeated Satan.

1 John 3:8 says, *"He that committeth sin is of the devil, for the devil sinneth from the beginning. For this purpose the Son of God was manifested that he might* ***destroy the works of the devil****."*

In Acts 26:18, Jesus speaks about His purpose for coming to earth, *"to open their eyes and to turn them from darkness to light and from the power of Satan unto God, that they may receive forgiveness of sins and inheritance among them which are sanctified by faith that is in me."*

Originally, God made Adam steward over the earth. But when Adam sinned, he handed stewardship to Satan, causing all mankind to fall under the devil's power. But Jesus redeemed the world. He restored our inheritance. Born-again believers are under the authority of Jesus and operate in His power. That's why we can defeat the devil.

Because that's true, we must take authority over Satan. Paul said in Galatians 2:20, *"I am crucified with Christ; nevertheless I live; yet not I but Christ liveth in me."* We are *new* creatures in Christ. Philippians 4:13 says, *"I can do all things through Christ which strengtheneth me."* The Bible tells us that Jesus is in us and we are in Him. And where is Jesus? He's sitting at the right hand of His Father. God told Him to, *"sit thou on my right hand til I make thine enemies thy footstool."* (Matthew 22:44) So, if we are in Jesus and are seated with him, where is Satan? **Under our feet!**

But too often we fail to dwell in heavenly places, in the spiritual realm, with eyes on God. Instead, like Elisha's servant in 2 Kings 6:11-17, our eyes are on our circumstances. Elisha's servant became fearful because he only saw the Syrian army surrounding him and not the far greater heavenly army. We need to keep focused on God and not our situation.

The Bible says we are more than conquerors. And more means more. 1 John 4:4 says, *"Ye are of God little children and have overcome them* (Overcome who? Satan and his fallen angles-the host of hell) *because greater is He that is in you, than he who is in the world."*

The Bible also tells us that, if God be for us who can be against us. God is rooting for us. He wants us to succeed. He has given us everything we need to be victorious in Him. That doesn't mean it will be easy or that we'll never have problems. It means when we do, God will see us through. He'll be right there strengthening, encouraging, and upholding us until we come out on the other side, victorious.

So, how do we take authority?

Ephesians 4:27 tells us not to, *"give place to the devil."* In other words, we are not to indulge our self-pity, our hurt feelings, our bad moods, etcetera. A toehold is all Satan needs to get us to take our eyes off God and put them on ourselves. And when we do, the spiral downward can be swift.

Ephesians 6:11 also tells us to, *"put on the whole armour of God."* And all eight steps are in order of necessary preparation, each building on the other, then finally working together.

First: *"having your loins girt about with truth."* That word "loins" means "hip, thigh, procreative power." There's that word "thigh" again! Our loins, our thighs, need to be "girted," to be fastened all around by truth. Jesus said in John 14:6, *"I am the* *way, the* ***truth****, the life: no man cometh unto the Father but by me."*

We've left Satan's family, and entered God's through Jesus. He surrounds and protects our thigh now. We've done our wrestling with Him and have surrendered and are willing to pay the price. And that means giving Jesus lordship over us. We no longer call the shots. He does. Before we can face off with Satan and overcome him, we must do this.

Second: *"having on the breastplate of righteousness."* The breastplate covers our chest, our heart. Jesus is our righteousness. He has become our personal Savior. Our hearts are now tied to His. We now care about the things He cares about. We concern ourselves with what concerns Him.

Third: *"And your feet shod with the preparation of the gospel of peace."* We're learning God's Word and are walking in it and sharing it with others.

Fourth: *"Above all taking the shield of faith, wherewith ye shall be able to quench all the fiery darts of the wicked."* God's Word builds up our faith. Without faith it is impossible to please God (Hebrews 11:6). It is faith that moves mountains. It's faith in God and in His promises that enables us to stand against the wiles of the devil.

Fifth: *"And take the helmet of salvation."* A helmet encircles the head. That word "salvation" here means "salvation, defender, defense." The mind is the battlefield. We must guard, defend and protect it. We are to keep our thoughts in check and guard what we dwell on. We must defend our mind from wrong or worldly thinking. This is vital. Proverbs 23:7 says as a man, *"thinketh in his heart so is he."* What fills our minds will eventually show up in our actions.

Sixth: *"And the sword of the Spirit, which is the Word of God."* A sword is used in battle. But that word "sword" here also means a knife, war, judicial punishment. The Word of God is the knife, the instrument of judicial punishment against Satan. When a situation comes up, we must speak God's Word over it. We speak those words that fit the situation. If we are sick, we can declare that by Jesus's stripes we are healed and that we are fearfully and wonderfully made, etcetera. That's our part. And when we speak God's Word of faith instead of our words of fear and doubt, we provide the Spirit of God with the weapon to use against Satan.

Our words are incredibly important. They can produce good as well as evil. Proverbs 18:21 says, *"death and life are in the power of the tongue."* We can curse ourselves and others by speaking negatively. Constantly telling someone, "you can't do anything right!" will plant destructive seeds in that person's life. First, he'll believe that he can't do anything right, and finally the self-fulfillment where he really *can't* do anything right!

Seventh: *"Praying always with all prayer and supplication in the Spirit."* We are to be in a constant attitude of prayer.

Eight: *"And watching thereunto with all perseverance and supplication for all saints."* We are now built up and ready to do spiritual battle and stand in the gap for others, especially believers.

Using our Weapons:

Our weapons are powerful and include the Word of God, the blood of Jesus, the name of Jesus, the word of our testimony and praise.

First, let's look at the Word of God. The Bible contains all of God's promises to us. The only way to be victorious is to stand on them in faith. But remember, Satan also knows Scripture and tries to twist and pervert it. We can't be like Eve. We can't add or detract from God's Word if we want to stand. We must live by the pure Word of God.

Then there's the blood of Jesus. We should cover ourselves and our family with the blood of Jesus every day. Demons are terrified of Jesus' blood. It's what defeated them on Calvary.

I'm reminded of a true story I heard years ago about a convict who was nothing but trouble until he accepted Jesus as Lord and Savior. But his former behavior made him hated by the warden. Because of this, he was often singled out for punishment for both real and contrived offenses. During one of those times, the convict was put in solitary confinement and visited by the warden and another prisoner who acted as an "enforcer," dispensing physical punishment to other prisoners on the warden's orders.

When the convict saw his fellow prisoner wearing brass knuckles, he knew he was in trouble. As a new Christian, he had learned only a few Scriptures, mostly about the blood of Jesus. And that was his only defense. After quickly covering himself with Jesus' blood, he kept mumbling, "the blood of Jesus, the blood of Jesus," during which time both the warden and the fellow prisoner began backing out of the cell, never laying a hand on him. It was the last time he and the warden had issues.

Then there's the name of Jesus which is a name above every name! Philippians 2:10 says, *"That at the name of Jesus every knee should bow, of things in heaven, and things in hearth, and things under the earth."* And that means Satan and all his minions!

The Bible also says that the name of Jesus is a, *"more excellent name,"* and we have the right to use it. When we do, all the power of Jesus goes with it. The Bible says we are ambassadors of Christ. When an earthly ambassador issues an official statement, his host country knows that all the power of that ambassador's country is behind it. So it is when we use the name of Jesus. All the power behind that name goes with it, too.

Here's another true story. A woman in a department store was trying on clothes in the dressing room when a man came bursting in with a knife to rob her. She rebuked him in the name of Jesus, which caused him to stand paralyzed while she escaped.

These stories may seem fantastic, but they're not isolated incidences. God is faithful and has promised to take care of His children. He has not left us defenseless.

In Matthew 16:19 Jesus said, *"I will give unto thee the keys of the kingdom of heaven and whatsoever thou shalt bind on earth shall be bound in heaven; and whatsoever thou shat loose on earth shall be loosed in heaven."*

This Scripture has been incorrectly used for forgiving sins. That word "bind" in Greek means "to be in bonds, knit, tie, wind." And that word "loose" means "to loosen, break, destroy, dissolve, melt, put off." This tells us that we have the power to bind Satan and loose ourselves from his curses, his power, etcetera. And we never, never do this in our own name but only in the name of Jesus. And in that name, we can cast out demons.

In Matthew 12:28-29 Jesus said, *"But if I cast out devils by the Spirit of God, then the kingdom of God is come unto you. Or else how can one enter into a strong man's house, and spoil his goods, except he first bind the strong man? And then he will spoil his house."* So, in the name of Jesus we bind Satan or the strongman over us. We loose ourselves from his power. We cover ourselves with the blood of Jesus. We ask the Holy Spirit to fill us and empower us. Then we surround ourselves with ministering angles to protect us. In other words, we are proactive!

Jesus confirms this in Matthew 11:12 when He said, *"from the days of John the Baptist until now the kingdom of heaven suffereth violence, and the violent take it by force."* That word "violent" is *biastes* is Greek and means "to press, forcer, energetic." If we want victory, it's going to take effort on our part. We need to press and strive spiritually for it.

Then there's the word of our testimony. Revelation 12:11 says, *"And they overcame him* (Satan) *by the blood of the Lamb, and by the word of their testimony."* Our testimony is what God has done in our life. And every time we share it with others, we give Satan indigestion.

Next, praise. Oh, how affective praise is! It puts things into prospective, namely that God is in control and we're not. It lifts us up when we feel down. It dislodges principalities and powers because God inhabits the praises of His people and His presence makes demons scatter.

And finally, we have ministering angles whose task is to protect and minister to us. Praise God!

How is Satan working in the world today?

It's obvious that Satan is more active than ever. Even non-believers feel something is wrong. Our society is losing its common decency. Things seem to be getting darker. Satan is stepping up his game both overtly and covertly; both as a powerful demonic entity and as an angel of light. And the more territory he takes, the darker it will get. How is he doing this? Here are some ways.

The occult. It's quickly gaining ground in our society.

Webster defines occult as: "hidden, secret, designating or of certain mystic arts or studies." Any involvement in these "secret arts" can open the door for Satan into our lives. The occult has already infiltrated our movies, television programs, books, schools, and even some churches. We must guard our own hearts and homes against it.

What are some of the doorways to the occult and by extension, demonic activity?

The list includes sorcery, wizardry, magic, witchcraft both white and black. Sorcery and wizardry are defined as the use of evil supernatural power over people and their affairs. Witchcraft is defined as the use of spells and incantations to control a person or event. Some high schools actually teach witchcraft as a subject! And look at the Harry Potter phenomenon. Since these books have come out, witchcraft sites have been bombarded with young people looking for information. Matthew 18:6 says, *"But whoso shall offend* (become a stumbling block, an evil influence to) *one of these little ones which believe in me, it were better for him that a millstone were hanged about his neck, and that he were drowned in the depth of the sea."*

It will not go well, on Judgment Day, for those who have led young believers away from the Lord and encouraged their dabbling in the occult!

Next, are various forms of divination such as fortune telling, horoscopes (they are in every major newspaper and even on line and people routinely read them thinking they are harmless), palm reading, water witching (finding underground water with a divining rod), tarot cards, tea leaf reading (I knew of Sister Mary, a nun for thirty years, who had someone come to the convent weekly to read tarot cards and tea leaves for her and the other sisters), numerology and the study of animal entrails.

There is also divination under the guise of science such as graphoanalysis which is hand writing analysis purporting to reveal a person's past and other information; iridology, a claim that just by looking into the iris of an eye any illness in that person's body can be diagnosed; applied kinesiology, which is the diagnosing of illness through muscle testing. True medical kinesiology is the study of human motion and is legitimate.

A doctor I went to, because he was also into vitamins and natural remedies, tried diagnosing me using kinesiology. He did this on two visits. The first time, it grieved my spirit and I didn't understand why. But by the second time, I realized this was a form of divination. I don't go to him anymore.

Then there's reflexology which supposedly can diagnose an illness from a person's reflexes. Hypnotism is another issue. It requires the submission of the person being hypnotized. It's basically a demonic trance. Sadly, techniques of self-hypnosis are currently being practiced in some of our public schools. 2 Corinthians 10:5 tells us to take every thought captive. We are to be in control of our minds and not allow others to control it. Demons often enter a person during hypnosis.

A case in point: while I was part of Women's Aglow, we had a guest speaker who was sick for twenty-five years after being hypnotized in a night club.

Acupuncture is another issue. It originated in Asia. Needles placed in certain areas are supposed to tap into the chi or spirit. And yes, they can provide healing, but a "demonic" healing. The purpose of acupuncture is specifically to arouse the kundalini force to bring about the healing of that person.

Acupressure is another one and works on the same principle as acupuncture.

Biofeedback produces a state of altered consciousness like meditation and self-hypnosis. All the above should be avoided.

Other occultic practices include contacting the dead (necromancy), séances, where a medium receives spirit communications from the dead. One of my husband's relatives went to a séance and the medium wouldn't proceed until he removed his cross and took the money out of his pocket because the bills said, "in God we trust." That should tell us all we need to know.

Consulting with familiar spirits is also demonic. Some Hollywood stars claim they channel "guides" who speak to them and give them information. What they are "channeling" are demonic spirits. The demonic spirits may give them information, even accurate information, but at what cost? Demonic co-habitation?

Transcendental meditation is another popular occultic practice. Visualization, guided imagery, Ouija boards and ESP (extra sensory perception) are others. When my children were in grade school, about thirty-five years ago, some of their required reading even then contained stories of clairvoyance and ESP. And according to an article in a Catholic magazine, ESP and mind control are taught in some Catholic schools.

Add to the list, astral projection (levitation), the New Age and the use of crystals.

Perhaps one of the biggest offenders of all is yoga because it is so popular and considered so benign. Yoga is NOT just physical exercise. There are two basic kinds: Kundalini yoga and tantra yoga.

The purpose of kundalini yoga is to arouse and control the kundalini force, the same kundalini force I mentioned in acupuncture. Kundalini literally means coiled and is named after the Hindu goddess symbolized by the serpent. This serpent allegedly resides in the body of a human near the base of the spine. When aroused with proper control, it supposedly brings strength, power and wisdom, as well as psychic abilities. The various yoga positions are designed to produce these results. This form of yoga is taught in gyms and many physical therapy departments.

Tantra yoga is popular in Europe, in corporations and in the medical field. It concentrates on powers, vibrations and energies. Some teachings of this also incorporate human sacrifice.

And let's not forget hard rock music. Sound waves can affect our brain as well as every cell in our body. Many hard rockers have made a pack with Satan, and that's a fact. Some, who have admitted this, say you can't get anywhere in hard rock unless you do. Some rock stars even make altar calls to Satan as well as perform animal sacrifices on stage.

Certain games such as Dungeons and Dragons, and a host of demonic video games have opened the door of many young hearts to the occult.

It shouldn't surprise us that we are seeing the rise of the occult. The religion of the antichrist will be occultic. This will also include drugs. It's interesting to note that most Satanic rituals involve drugs. Revelation 9:20-21 says that they repented not of their worship of devils, idols, their murders, thefts, fornication and **sorceries**. There are at least twenty-seven references to sorcery and witchcraft in the Bible and five are relate to drug use. Revelation 9:21 is one of them. That word "sorceries" here in Greek is *pharmakeia* from which we get the word pharmacy, meaning they did not repent of their drug use.

Even now, some politicians boldly claim they've experimented with them. Years ago, no politician would dare admit such a thing! It would have been a disqualifier. But today, it hardly phases, and some even think it's "cool." Oh, how far we have fallen!

So, we see why the world is getting darker. It's due to the increase and acceptance of occultic practices. When people stray from Biblical moorings, Satan and his crowd will happily fill the void.

And here's a word of caution: just believing that any or all the above are okay, that there's nothing wrong with them, will not protect someone from their consequences. That speaker at the Aglow meeting didn't think being hypnotized by a performer in a night club would hurt. After all, it was just harmless fun. But for twenty-five years she suffered from one sickness after the other until she came to the Lord and He showed her how a spirit of infirmity had gained access to her during hypnosis.

What does the Bible say about these things?

Deuteronomy 18:10-12 says, *"There shall not be found among you any one that maketh his son or his daughter to pass through the fire* (become a human sacrifice) *or that useth divination, or an observer of times, or an enchanter, or a witch, or a charmer, or a consulter with familiar spirits or a wizard, or a necromancer. For all that do these things are an* ***abomination*** *unto the LORD; and because of these abominations the LORD thy God doth drive them out from before thee."*

God says these things are an abomination. They are the very reason He drove out the Canaanites and others for Israel.

Leviticus 20:6 warns, *"And the soul that turneth after such as have familiar spirits, and after wizards, to go a whoring after them, I will even set my face against that soul, and will cut him off from among his people."*

In Deuteronomy 4:16-19 God condemns all idolatry including worship of the heavenly bodies such as the sun, moon and stars, as in astrology and the reading of horoscopes.

Isaiah 47:10-15 talks about God's judgments on Babylon for their wickedness and for consulting evil spirits, for their enchantments, their sorceries, for seeking astrologers and stargazers, and says He will destroy them because of it.

There is a price for doing these things. God allows evil to come upon those who trust in or seek the power given them by evil spirits, and He says that disaster is in their future.

There are other references not listed, but the ones above should be enough to convince anyone that God HATES these occult practices, and that they carry dire consequences.

Satanic practices are becoming bolder and more open.

Why is the church so ineffective against Satan's onslaught? Because we look too much like the world. Because we have accepted too much worldly thinking. And because we are participating too much in the sins of the world, including dabbling in the occult and calling it "harmless."

Some Protestant ministers are even blatantly denying the deity of Jesus and the validity of the Bible. By doing this, they are opening the door for Satan to come into their churches with some of his own goodies. And he's not shy. He'll gladly do it.

And nothing typifies society's downward spiral better than Halloween. Though it's been around forever, it's becoming increasingly darker. It's viewed as a fun holiday by non-Christians as well as many Christians. It's an important holiday for Satan and includes vile acts and rituals performed by occultists. Even the innocent are often affected when they go to a Halloween party and are put into a trance or coerced into making vows to Satan as a joke. It's happening, folks, every year. We need to wake up.

And we can't forget our young children. Satan hasn't. More and more children's programs and cartoons now include witches, wizards, sorcerers, aliens, and creatures that are part human and part alien, all portrayed in a positive light, all preparing the next generation for the occult.

Because these things are becoming more accepted, more mainstream, more people are buying the lie and becoming entrapped. At first it seems all fun-and-games, then reality sets in. Several years ago, a woman from England was the guest on a popular Christian television show. She explained how when she was a prostitute, she became involved in white witchcraft just for fun. But the more she got into it, the more it got her. She eventually switched from white to black magic, became one of England's most powerful witches, was impregnated by a warlock, then offered her baby as a human sacrifice to Satan. Mercifully, sometime after the death of her child, Jesus appeared to her and set her free.

The Bible tells us that Satan can come as an *"angel of light."* He will try to fool and seduce us. We must be vigilant not only for ourselves but our families. We must allow the Word of God to transform our worldly attitudes, including those regarding the occult. Hosea 4:6 says, *"My people are destroyed for lack of knowledge."* We must not let that be said about us. Satan is real and the occult is NOT harmless. We must take them both seriously.

Question Ten: *What about hell?*

"If God is so loving, how could He create hell?"

God never intended that man should go to hell. Initially, it was created for Satan and the fallen angels. In Isaiah 14:12-14 Satan boastfully lists his five "I wills" saying how he was going to be like God. In verse 15, God responds by telling him, *"Yet thou shalt be brought down to hell, to the sides of the pit."* And 2 Peter 2:4 talks about how God didn't spare the angels who sinned and cast them into hell where they are currently chained.

At present, not all fallen angels are in hell. According to Jude 6, those in hell are the ones who left their first estate. *"And the angels which kept not their first estate but left their own habitation, he hath reserved in everlasting chains under darkness unto the judgment of the great day."* Who are these angels? They are the, *"sons of God"* who *"saw the daughters of men that they were fair; and they took them wives of all which they chose."* (Genesis 6:2) These are the angles who fathered the giants of old, the very ones of Greek mythology. But that's for another study.

But when man sinned, hell became his destination, too. Psalms 9:17 says, *"The wicked shall be turned into hell, and all the nations that forget God."* But God is merciful. Those who love Him and serve Him have always had a way of escape. My book, **Following the Blood Trail from Genesis to Revelation** covers this in detail.

So, we see that hell is for Satan and the fallen angels, as well as fallen, unrepentant man.

What is hell like?

Jesus describes it in Mark 9:43-48. He calls it a, *"fire that never shall be quenched; Where their worm dieth not, and the fire is not quenched."* If we were to read all the verses (43-48) we'd see that four times Jesus mentions the fire will never be quenched. In other words, it will burn for all eternity, indicating that those who are in hell will be there for all eternity. Also, in Mark 9, Jesus says if our hand, foot or eye causes us to sin it's better to cut them off (hand/foot) or pluck it out (eye). He didn't mean we should literally do it. Rather, He was making a point. He wanted everyone to know that hell was so terrible it should be avoided at all cost. This is repeated in Matthew 5:29-30 and Matthew 18:8-9.

Several books have been written by those who claim to have gone to hell and returned. And they all have one thing in common, the description. They talk about the horrible smell, the suffocating heat, and people screaming in agony. No one, to my knowledge, has ever described it as a happy or pleasant place. I think it's safe to say that our worst day on earth would be better than the best day in hell.

Jesus spoke of hell often. In Matthew 23:15, He calls the scribes and Pharisees, *"child of hell."* In verse 33, He calls them serpents and vipers and asks them how they expected to, *"escape the damnation of hell?"*

Jesus never minced words. In Matthew 10:28, He tells His disciples, *"fear not them which kill the body, but are not able to kill the soul: but rather fear him* (God) *which is able to destroy both soul and body in hell."* In Luke 12:5 He says something similar. *"But I will forewarn you whom ye shall fear: Fear him which after he hath killed hath power to cast into hell; yea, I say unto you, Fear him."*

I doubt we can even imagine what hell is like. But certainly, it's more horrible and terrifying than the worst vision we could ever conceive. But the thing is, we don't have to go there. God has always provided a way of escape. For those in the Old

Testament, it meant animal sacrifices. For us, it means Jesus.

Jesus said in Revelation 3:5, *"He that overcometh, the same shall be clothed in white raiment; and I will not blot out his name out of the book of life, but I will confess his name before my Father, and before his angels."* All overcomers in Jesus will be spared hell.

In Revelation 1:18, Jesus declares that he has, *"the keys of hell and of death."* Why? Because He defeated them both on Calvary. In Matthew 16:18b, Jesus promises that, *"the gates of hell shall not prevail against it."* Against what? Against His church, meaning those who believe in Him. Hell, and the second death (God's White Throne Judgment where people will be *"cast into the lake of fire"* Revelation 20:15) no longer have power over believers.

Who will go to hell?

Aside from Satan and the fallen angels, Revelation 20:15 tells us that, *"whosoever was not found written in the book of life was cast into the lake of fire."* Oh, dear. If that's so, then we should all want our names written in it!

The Bible speaks of the unpardonable sin as blaspheming the Holy Spirit. Obviously, those not written in the book of life have blasphemed the Holy Spirit by rejecting His continuous revelation that Jesus is the Son of God and our Savior.

Can Christians go to hell?

Before going further, that word "Christian" must be defined. If the question is being asked about **cultural** Christians, those who say they are Christian because their parents are or because they may attend church on Easter and Christmas, then yes, hell is in their future. Why? Because they are Christians in name only. I understand these people. I was one of them.

And if the question is asked about **carnal** Christians, those who mouthed the sinner's prayer, giving it lip service but not coming from the heart, and whose lives have never changed but still mimic those in the world with no regard for God or His Word, then yes, hell is their destination, too.

But if we are taking about a genuine **born-again** Christian, regardless of denomination, one who has surrendered and made Jesus his Lord and Savior, then that question becomes more difficult to answer. And exploring it feels a bit like wading into quicksand. But I'll address it later.

So, not everyone who **thinks** he is a Christian will go to heaven. Just thinking we are a Christian because we've been baptized into a church or attend services periodically or try to follow our church's rules does not make us a genuine Christian. Church doesn't save us, Jesus does. Neither does mouthing a quick insincere sinner's prayer.

Matthew 7:15-16 says, *"Beware of false prophets, which come to you in sheep's clothing, but inwardly they are ravening wolves. Ye shall know them by their fruits."* This Scripture specifically references false prophets, indicating that not everyone claiming to be a prophet, is one. God certainly knows who they are, just as He knows the true believers from those who just claim to be.

In Matthew 7:21-23, Jesus gives a stern warning, *"Not every one that saith unto me, Lord, Lord, shall enter into the kingdom of heaven;* ***but he that doeth the will of my Father*** *which is in heaven. Many will say to me in that day* (the day of judgment) *Lord, Lord, have we not prophesied in thy name? and in thy name have cast out devils? and in thy name done many wonderful works? And then will I profess unto them, I never knew you; depart from me, ye that work iniquity."* Jesus looks at the heart. Our good deeds don't fool Him. He knows who's genuine and who's not.

Relationship, not attending an organized church, makes a Christian. A genuine Christian is one who has acknowledged he is a sinner, has accepted Jesus as Savior, has acknowledged that it's only Jesus' blood sacrifice that restores him to God the Father and therefore has a relationship with Him.

In Revelation 3:5, Jesus said, *"He that overcometh, the same shall be clothed in white raiment; and I will not blot out his name out of the book of life."* And remember what Revelation 20:15 told us? *"Whosoever was not found written in the book of life was cast into the lake of fire."*

So, anyone NOT written in the book of life will go to hell. The Bible can't be any clearer!

How can a genuine Christian be blotted out?

I want to tread carefully here. God's grace is an incredibly wonderful thing. His blood pays for all our sins: past, present and future. And there is no sin too great God can't or won't forgive if we confess it and repent. But I fear that the current teaching of "hyper grace" can lead believers astray. Grace does not give us license to live anyway we want. God is holy and we are called to live holy lives, too, submitted and obedient to Him.

Galatians 6:7 says, *"Be not deceived; God is not mocked: for whatsoever a man soweth, that shall he also reap."* There is no fooling God. Our fruits will always give us away.

But can a genuine Christian, one who isn't prefect but who loves God and tries to live a holy life, go to hell? I believe the one thing that can derail a genuine Christian is unforgiveness and perhaps even keep him from heaven. Why? Because Jesus Himself said, *"For **if ye forgive** men their trespasses, your heavenly Father will also forgive you; But **if ye forgive not** men their trespasses, neither will your Father forgive your trespasses."*

The whole reason we, as born-again believers, have assurance of heaven is that we are forgiven, and our sins are covered by the blood of Jesus. But here, Jesus is saying that our sins are **NOT** forgiven if we don't forgive others.

Again, in Matthew 18:23-35 Jesus talks about a king who began tallying the accounts of his servants. One servant owed him a great deal of money, yet the king forgave him his debt. But this same servant, who was owed a small sum by a fellow servant, refused to forgive that servant. Jesus then, in verse 34, tells how the king reacted. *"And his lord was wroth, and delivered him* (the servant who had owed him a lot of money) *to the tormentors, till he should pay all that was due unto him."*

In Mark 11:25-26, Jesus says, *"And when ye stand praying,* ***forgive****, if ye have ought against any: that your Father also which is in heaven may* ***forgive*** *you your trespasses. But if ye do not* ***forgive****, neither will your Father which is in heaven* ***forgive*** *your trespasses."* If our sins are not forgiven by God then we are considered sinners, and no sinner will enter the kingdom of heaven!

Jesus continues this theme in Luke 6:37. *"Judge not, and ye shall not be judged: condemn not, and ye shall not be condemned:* ***forgive****, and ye shall be* ***forgiven****."*

When Jesus was teaching His disciples the Lord's prayer, He said in Luke 11:4, *"And* ***forgive us*** *our sins;* ***for we also forgive every one*** *that is indebted to us."* Again, God's forgiving us is tied to us forgiving others. No forgiveness for others, then no forgiveness for us.

Remember Revelation 3:5? Jesus said, *"He that overcometh, the same shall be clothed in white raiment; and I will not* ***blot out*** *his name out of the book of life."* Here, Jesus indicates it's possible to be blotted out of the book of life! And what then? *"Whosoever was not found written in the book of life was cast into the lake* *of fire."* Let that not happen to us because of unforgiveness.

We have no right to keep grudges or maintain a heart of unforgiveness. Jesus is like that king in Matthew 18 who has forgiven us much (a large sum). Dare we not forgive others their small sum? It's up to God to settle the accounts. Romans 12:19b says, *"Vengeance is mine; I Will repay, saith the Lord."* So, let's leave it to Him.

While I was struggling with this issue, I happened to see a Christian program where an African pastor was relaying an amazing story, a story documented and certified by his community. He had had an argument with his wife and had been rejecting her apologies, refusing to forgive her as well as punishing her with the silent treatment for nearly a week. At the end of it, he had a terrible car accident resulting in a death experience and found himself in hell. He described the horror of it and how he cried out to God that this had to be a mistake. He was a pastor and a true lover of God. An angel appeared to him and told him if God were to leave him in this state of death, hell would be his eternal home. Because he refused to forgive his wife, God could not forgive him. The pastor immediately repented and found himself on a slab in the morgue.

We are not required or expected to accept every Christian's supernatural experience as fact, so believe or not as you will. But it does give food for thought as well as give the above Scriptures a startling and horrifying sense of realism.

In conclusion:

It's not our job to look at the people in our church and try to determine who does and doesn't go to heaven. Only God knows the heart. Only He knows who is genuine and who isn't. Only He knows if someone has disqualified himself. So, we must leave judgment to Him. However, regarding our fitness for heaven, if there are any take-aways I'd like to leave, here they are:

1. Maintain a close relationship with God
2. Live as holy a life as possible
3. Confess sins quickly
4. Don't hold grudges, but walk in instant forgiveness
5. Understand there is no guarantee that our life will extend past the present second. We could meet Jesus at any moment. Be ready!

Question Eleven: *Are we in the end times?*

"And if so, does that mean the world will end?"

Regarding whether the world will end:

At first glance, the Bible may seem contradictory because the translators often translated "landmass," "age" (a specific season or time) and "everlasting" into "earth or world," causing confusion. Let's look at some examples.

Psalms 104:5 says, *"Who laid the foundations of the* ***earth*** *that it should not be removed for ever."* That word "earth" in Hebrew is *erets* and means a physical landmass. *Erets* is also the same word for "earth" in Ecclesiastes 1:4. *"One generation passeth away, and another generation cometh; but the* ***earth*** *abideth for ever."*

But when Isaiah 45:17 mentions the ***"world without end"*** that word "world" in Hebrew is *olam,* meaning "eternity, everlasting, to hide in a distant future." So, when Isaiah says, *"But Israel shall be saved in the*

*LORD with an everlasting salvation; ye shall not be ashamed nor confounded **world without end**,"* it's saying that Israel shall be saved and unashamed for all eternity.

When Paul says in Ephesians 3:21, *"Unto him be glory in the church by Christ Jesus throughout all ages, **world without end**,"* that word "world" is *aion* in Greek, and means "an age, a specific time period." So, what Paul is saying is that Jesus and His church will be glorified in an age without end, in other words, eternity.

In Mark 13:31, Jesus says, *"Heaven and **earth** shall pass away: but my words shall not pass away."* Here, that word "earth" in Greek is *ge* and means "soil, globe, land, ground." So, at some point the literal globe, the land will pass away. Jesus said something similar in Matthew 5:18, *"For verily I say unto you, Till heaven and **earth** pass, one jot or one tittle shall in no wise pass from the law, till all be fulfilled"*. Again, that word "earth" is *ge*.

When His disciples ask Jesus in Matthew 24:3b, *"what shall be the sign of thy coming, and of the end of the **world**?"* that word is *aion*, meaning "age." So, the disciples were asking when the end of the age would be, and not the end of the world. And when Jesus said in Matthew 13:39b, *"the harvest is the end* *of the* ***world****; and the reapers are the angels"* again that word is *aion* and Jesus is speaking about the end of the age, the end of a specific time frame.

Let's put it together.

Scripture indicates that this age we are living in will not last forever, while the earth, in some form, will. Revelation 20:11 says, *"And I saw a great white throne, and him that sat on it, from whose face the* ***earth*** *and the heaven fled away; and there was found no place for them."* Revelation 21:1 continues this theme. *"And I saw a new heaven and a new* ***earth****; for the first heaven and the first* ***earth*** *were passed away; and there was no more sea."*

The Greek word *ge* is used all three times for "earth" in the above Scriptures. Remember, *ge* means "soil, a globe, land, ground." And that word "passed" is *parerchomai* in Greek and means "to come near, aside, go away, perish, neglect." So, at some point, God will replace the old earth with a new earth. Why and how, we leave to Him.

Having established that the earth, in some form, will continue to exist, let's address the question of whether we are in the end times.

A short answer is, yes. However, even the disciples believed they were in the last days or end times. It could be said that we have been in the end times for nearly 2000 years! But I believe we are in the "end" of the end times.

Okay, so why bother knowing about the end times?

In Luke 12:54-56, Jesus rebuked the people for knowing the weather by the signs in the sky, but not knowing the signs of His day, and called them "hypocrites." Prophecy makes up about 27% of the Bible. To ignore it would be to literally ignore one-fourth of the Bible!

Ed Hindson, noted Bible prophecy teacher, former host of the *King is Coming* television program, and instructor at Liberty University said, "Prophecy is not meant to scare us but to prepare us."

It's also a great witnessing tool. As the signs of the times unfold, people will want answers. This will provide an opening for us to tell them about Bible prophecy and Jesus.

How does the Bible describe the end times?

2 Timothy 3:1-4 gives us the glum picture. *"This know also, that in the last days perilous times shall come. For men shall be lovers of their own selves, covetous,*

boasters, proud, blasphemers, disobedient to parents, unthankful, unholy, Without natural affection, trucebreakers, false accusers, incontinent, fierce, despisers of those that are good, Traitors, heady, high-minded, lovers of pleasures more than lovers of God."

From this, we see that the end times will be dangerous and punctuated by extreme selfishness. If that doesn't describe our society today, I don't know what does.

Jesus, in Matthew 24:1-12, gives additional signs which include: wars, rumors of wars, famines, pestilences and earthquakes, persecution of believers, the rise of false prophets, deception in the church, false signs and wonders, and signs in the heavens.

You may be thinking, *but nothing has changed. We've always experienced these things throughout history.* True. But now they are increasing and converging. In other words, they are happening all at once and with more intensity.

Where is America right now?

Deuteronomy 19:15b tells us that, *"at the mouth of two witnesses, or at the mouth of three witnesses, shall the matter be established,"* and 2 Corinthians 13:1b says, *"in the mouth of two or three witnesses shall every word be established."* This means that at least two witnesses must establish a word or matter.

Has God sent at least two witnessed to prophecy against America? Actually, more. But I will only mention two:

The first witness is Shane Warren, Senior Pastor of The Assembly in West Monroe, Louisiana, an author and president of The Voice Network. God gave him a vision of a huge hurricane covering the entire U.S. where money, instead of rain, fell. It was a picture of the dollar becoming worthless. He saw riots in the streets much like the kind we've seen in Europe, and mobs demanding their "entitlements."

America is at a tipping point due to her immorality. Warren discussed the four winds blowing to create a perfect storm: politics, economics, religion and war. God will use all four to shake America.

The second witness I will mention is Jonathan Cahn, an author and messianic Jewish pastor of Hope of the World Ministries and the Jerusalem Center/Beth Israel in New Jersey.

In Cahn's book, *The Harbinger*, he shares the insights God gave him regarding the 9/11 terrorist attack, an attack paralleling what happened to ancient Israel as revealed through Isaiah 9:10-21. I will not detail the book here, but it is incredibly insightful; a warning that our hedge of protection has been lifted. I highly recommend his book for those desiring more specifics.

In his next book, *The Mystery of the Shemitah*, Cahn details further parallels between Israel and America regarding God's judgment. Another great read.

The takeaway in both is that just as Israel turned from God and was punished, so has America turned from God, and His judgment is at our very door.

Let's look at the four winds: politics, economics, religion and war.

World Politics:

The world is a mess. That's plain to see. And amid all the chaos, the stage is being set for a One World Government. Satan has been trying to set up a One World Government since the Tower of Babel. Why? Because it's easier to control nations if they fall under one government.

Throughout history, Satan has had someone in the wings to take over the world or try to; men like

Nimrod, Nebuchadnezzar, Alexander the Great, just to mention a few. In modern times, he had Adolph Hitler who claimed his Third Reich would last 1000 years—a blasphemous boast mimicking Jesus' promised 1000-year reign.

Jack Van Impe does a great job in laying out the background of the New World Order in his DVD, *New World Order Rising*. In it, he exposes the seven organizations that are working to create this order.

First: The Illuminati, began in ancient Egypt under the Rosicrucians. In 1771 they reemerged in Europe to promote a One World Order. Karl Marx, the father of Communism, came out of the Illuminati. Their insignia is on the back of the U.S. dollar: a pyramid and an all-seeing eye.

The top ranks of the Freemans (33rd degree Masons) are associated with the illuminati. In addition, six other organizations have come out of the illuminati: The Council on Foreign Relations, the UN, the Bilderbergs, the Club of Rome, the Trilateral Commission, and the New Age Movement. They make up the remaining six discussed below.

Second: The Council on Foreign Relations, began in 1921 and which has worked hard to get the United States to back the idea of a One World Government.

Third: The UN, which was founded in 1945. In 1980, it formulated a plan for the New World Order. In 1996 it detailed how to implement this plan in a 420-page document entitled, *Our Global Neighborhood.*

While no cross or other religious artifacts are displayed in or on UN grounds, a statue of Zeus is near the entrance of the main lobby. The statue has been acknowledged as being that of Zeus since 1953 when the Greek government gifted it to the UN. But recently, the UN claimed it's really a statue of Poseidon. What? Why the change?

Could it be because Zeus was referred to as "Satan" by Jesus in a letter where He said the seat of Satan was in Pergamos? The seat Jesus referenced was the throne or altar of Zeus (Revelation 2:12-13). In 1930, this throne was dismantled and taken to Berlin, Germany where it currently resides in the Berlin Pergamon Museum. Perhaps the UN doesn't want this connection to their statue known and hopes to cover it up. If so, it would speak volumes.

Fourth: The Bilderbergs, began 1954 in Holland. A secretive organization, it's behind the European Union. They wanted to have everyone in the world implanted with a microchip by 2017. Obviously, they are behind schedule.

Fifth: The Club of Rome, began in 1968. In 1974, it released a plan to divide the world into ten political and economic regions. That reminds me of the ten toes in the book of Daniel.

Here are the designated zones:

1. America, Canada, Mexico. Perhaps this is why so many in the U.S. government are unwilling to secure our boarders and do anything on immigration reform.
2. South and Central America
3. Australia and New Zealand
4. Western Europe
5. Eastern Europe
6. Japan
7. South Asia
8. Central Asia
9. North Africa and Middle East
10. the rest of Africa

Sixth: The Trilateral Commission began in 1973 by David Rockefeller. It was initially founded to encourage interaction and cooperation among the U.S., western Europe and Japan. Mentioned in its founding declaration is this quote, "Growing interdependence is a fact of life of the contemporary world. It **transcends** and influences national systems."

Note the word "transcends." Webster defines it as "to be superior, surpass, excel." In other words, this interdependence is more important and is above the national sovereignty of any nation. According to Revelation 13:17, the antichrist will be in total control of the world's economic system. No one will be able to buy or sell without his mark. In order to "transcend" a nation's sovereignty, the need for a One World Government is implied.

Seventh: The New Age Movement. David Spangler, a leader in the movement, was told by his spirit guide to prepare for the New World Order and that their messiah, whose number is 666, will appear soon in bodily form.

Many of the "movers and shakers" of our world (bankers, media members, corporate executives, politicians and heads of state) are part of one or more of these organizations. Nelsen Rockefeller, Richard Nixon, John Kennedy, and George Bush Sr. all called for a New World Order. In 1975, thirty-two U.S. Senators and ninety-two U.S. Representatives signed a "Declaration of Independence" stating, "we must bring forth a New World Order." One can only imagine how much that number has grown!

World Economics:

Many countries are carrying way too much debt and are on the verge of bankruptcy. Even America is facing a financial cliff. All this debt in our country and others is **UNSUSTAINABLE**.

Right now, the U.S. dollar and four others (China yuan, British pound, Japanese yen and Euro) are the global reserve currencies. And the dollar is also the only currency by which countries can buy oil. For years, China, Russia and several other nations have talked about dumping the dollar. They want to create a new global currency. In the meantime, China has been busily buying up gold. That should tell us something.

When the dollar is dumped, it will create a financial free fall in the U.S. This mimics Shane Warren's vision of the dollar falling and the ensuing riots. Because the US is already on the financial brink, with its trillions in debt, it wouldn't take much to push it over the edge.

There is already talk of creating a one world currency. In July of 2009, at the G-8 Summit, then Russian President Medvedev predicted a coming global currency. He promptly displayed the new global coin which was minted in Brussels. On the front was inscribed, "Unity in Diversity." The back said, "United Future World Currency." Though nothing has come of it, it's certainly symbolic of what *is* coming.

Now, let's look at religion.

In America and elsewhere, more and more churches no longer preach the full gospel. Instead, it's a watered-down version designed to offend no one. In addition, some are preaching "replacement theology" which claims that God is finished with Israel and has replaced her with the church. Replacement theology further claims that all Scriptures mentioning Israel actually apply to the church. When reading it that way, one must literally twist into knots to make it sound even remotely plausible.

In June 2011, the World Council of Churches met in Bolos Greece to discuss the growing number of Christians murdered at the hands of Muslims. And what was their conclusion? *Israel was responsible!* Furthermore, they declared the Jewish state a "sin"! If that weren't enough, they went on to say that Christians had the responsibility to resist this "offensive" Jewish existence.

The above demonstrates an irrational hatred of Jews and Israel, and is blatantly anti-Semitic. Let me be clear, antisemitism is demonically inspired. Satan hates the Jews because from them came God's Word and commandments, as well as the New Testament and Messiah, Jesus—the cause of Satan's defeat at the cross.

Satan is also behind all the fuss, tensions and disputes over Israel's land, especially Jerusalem. This land is about the size of New Jersey and looks like a sliver on the map. So why would Satan want the world to get bent out of shape over such a small parcel? Because, as the current god of this world, he wants his man, the antichrist, to be in Jerusalem when he announces his supposed divinity and subsequent demand to be worshipped. Jerusalem is the very place where Jesus will return to earth and set up His 1000-year reign. It's just another one of Satan's attempts to counterfeit the things of God.

Another problem area is the UN which is actively promoting "religious pluralism," another word for a one world religion. Working closely with them is the World Council of Churches.

Then there's the rise of Chrislam. On June 26, 2011, U.S. churches in thirty-two states held "unity meetings" between Christianity and Islam, and placed the writings of the Quran and Bible on equal footing. They declared both books honor Jesus even though the prophet, Jesus, in the Quran has no resemblance to our Jesus. According to Islam, Jesus is **Not** the Son of God, **Not** virgin born, and **Never** died on the cross.

Muhammad Hisham Kabbani, Founder/Chairman of the Islamic Supreme Council of America, explains his Jesus this way: Jesus will return with the Muslim Messiah, Mahdi, to establish a New World Order. When he does, he will confess that he never died on the cross, that it was all a fake. He will further confess that while he was away, he discovered the truth of Islam. Then, he will destroy all crosses and become the Mahdi's executioner of every man, woman and child who does not convert to Islam.

To say their prophet Jesus is the same as our Jesus of the Bible is utter blasphemy! So is trying to co-mingle Islam with Christianity.

Next, consider the Catholic Church's role. Vatican II opened its door for a one world religion with its ecumenicalism. In 1982, Pope John Paul II had a prayer meeting in Assisi, Italy which included pagans and voodoo priests, and where he claimed that voodoo possessed "truth and good, seeds of the Word."

And finally, there's the rise of secular humanism which has already been declared a "religion." Its primary tenant is to create a global society and to establish a social and economic order for the redistribution of wealth. It rejects the human need for salvation and believes Christian salvation to be "harmful."

So, what we are seeing here the seeds of a one world religion. The world is getting ready for antichrist. It's interesting to note that the three major world religions, Christianity, Judaism and Islam, are now all awaiting their messiah.

Wars:

Wars and rumors of wars abound. We see fighting everywhere, between neighbors, tribes, ethnic groups, countries. No one seems to be able to get along. The Middle East is a tinder box that could go up any second. In the fall of 2011, Major General Eyal Eisenberg, chief of the Israeli army's Home Front Command, said that because of the Arab Spring Israel could face a multi-front war.

Since then, they have been preparing for it. And the Israelis will fight to the death if they must. They have a "Samson Option" in which they are prepared to use nuclear weapons even if it means their own destruction. If they do use them, it could bring about a chain reaction. The sad part is that in the past, the U.S. has exacerbated this problem. Aside from Israel's Muslim enemies, no one has done more to try to divide the land of Israel than the U.S. God forgive us! In many ways, it has left war as the only remaining option for Israel.

Iran continues to sponsor terrorism, especially against Israel. If they push too hard, Israel will have no alternative but to push back. The Bible describes the wars of Psalms 83 and Ezekiel 38 between Israel and her enemies. While these wars have yet to occur, many believe they could take place in the near future.

World reaction:

The world knows it's in trouble on all four fronts, politically, economically, spiritually, and militarily. That's why prophecies, like those in 2012 which predicted the end of the world, captured so much attention, especially Hollywood's. Even now, prophesies of the world ending, abound. And Hollywood continues to pump out apocalyptic-type movies.

But Romans 5:20 tells us that where sin abounds, grace abounds much more. We need not be afraid.

God is with us and will supply us with all the courage, fortitude and grace we need to face whatever the future brings. He will be our shield and protector, our provider and present help in times of trouble. But we do need to know what's happening so we can use our knowledge as a witnessing tool. And as the body of Christ, we must continue to repent, turn from our wicked ways, seek God's face and pray (2 Chronicles 7:14).

Question Twelve: Is there really going to be a rapture?

The rapture question garners more discord and anger than most other questions. And this puzzles me since it doesn't affect one's salvation, no matter what a person's view on it. I think sometimes this vitriol stems from a mistaken belief that rapture adherents will lead people into error, make them careless Christians and leave them unprepared for the Tribulation. I believe the opposite is true. If one believes that Jesus could come at any moment to collect His bride, that person is more likely to live his life all out for God.

Another common indictment concerns the very word "rapture." Since it's not in the Bible, it must be invalid or even heresy. But many other commonly accepted words such as Christianity, Trinity and Bible, are not mentioned, either. And while the word "rapture" may not explicitly be in Scripture, it is implied. In 1 Thessalonians 4:17, where it speaks of the rapture, it uses the term "caught up" which is *harpazo* in Greek and means "to seize, catch, pluck, pull, take by force." But when *harpazo* was translated into Latin, it became the word *rapiemur* which translates to "rapture" in English.

But putting that aside, to answer the question, yes, there is really going to be a rapture which, by extension, brings us to the next question. When?

There are three main theories

as well as a few minor ones. The three major ones claim the rapture will occur pre-Trib, mid-Trib or post-Tribulation. Pre-Tribulation rapture believers say the rapture will occur before the Tribulation begins. Mid-Tribers say it will happen in the middle, and post-Tribers believe it will happen at the end when we are caught up in the air, then do an immediate about-face and return to earth with Jesus.

The rapture should not be confused with the Second Coming of Christ. That's where some people miss it. They lump these two occurrences together. The second coming of Jesus is preceded by a series of specific signs, the rapture is not. There's not one sign, given in the Bible, that needs to be fulfilled prior to the rapture. Rather, it's imminent, meaning it could happen any time. And I believe this will happen prior to the Tribulation therefore I'm a pretribulationist.

With all this confusion, why study the rapture at all?

Because the Bible calls it, *"that blessed hope"* (Titus 2:13) and it's meant to encourage us. Also, it reminds us that we always need to be prepared to meet the Lord, to live our lives fully for Him. In addition, we can use it to encourage others. And finally, considering how terrible the Tribulation will be and how wonderful the pre-Tribulation rapture will be, it's an added incentive to pray diligently for others so they will be spared having to endure such a horrible time in history.

What did the apostles and early church fathers believe?

Ken Johnson, Th. D., author, lecturer of Bible prophecy and ancient history, addresses this in his book, *Ancient Church Fathers, What the Disciples of the Apostles Taught*. In it, he documents how not one ancient church father taught a mid-Tribulation or post-Tribulation rapture. While, on the other hand, many taught and wrote of a pre-Tribulation rapture such as:

- Shepherd of Hermas 150 A.D.—the name of a respected and popular Christian document
- Irenaeus 170 A.D.—Bishop of Lyons, France

- Tertullian 207 A.D.—presbyter in Carthage, North Africa
- Cyprian 250 A.D.—Bishop in Carthage, North Africa
- Ephraim the Syrian 373 A.D.—the name of a respected Christian document

The apostles and disciples themselves believed they were living in the end times and that the rapture would take place before the Tribulation and before Jesus' return as King of Kings and Lord of Lords. As mentioned, this belief was widely accepted in the early church.

Many disciples even believed Jesus would rapture the church before John the apostle died because Jesus told them in Matthew 16:28 that some would not die before seeing the Son of Man coming into His kingdom. They didn't understand that John would see this Kingdom in a revelation on the Island of Patmos.

So, what changed? In 70 A.D., Jerusalem was destroyed, and the Jews dispersed. Years went by, the apostles died, Israel remained scattered, and still no rapture. So, the church began to allegorize Revelation and the rapture teaching, saying it was a story revealing spiritual truths but not meant to be taken literally. They did this because they had no other way to explain it. This idea gradually took hold.

Then, in the 5th Century, St. Augustine, a prominent theologian of the Catholic Church, established his doctrine of amillennialism which claimed the age he was living in was the Millennium. He asserted that the Tribulation, in fact, had already occurred. Israel was no longer relevant, and the church would progressively purify the world. When it was sufficiently purified, Jesus would return. After Augustine, other theories emerged.

What does the Bible say?

Paul was given the mystery of the rapture. In 1 Corinthians 15:51-52 he said, *"Behold, I shew you a mystery; we shall not all sleep, but we shall all be changed, in a moment, in the twinkling of an eye, at the last trump: for the trumpet shall sound, and the dead shall be raised incorruptible, and we shall be changed."*

In 1 Thessalonians 4:16-17 Paul further describes this event. *"For the Lord Himself shall descend from heaven with a shout, with the voice of the archangel, and with the trump of God: And the dead in Christ shall rise first: Then we which are alive and remain shall be caught up together with them in the clouds, to meet the Lord in the air: and so shall we ever be with the Lord."*

This clearly tells us that Jesus does not return to earth during the rapture. But at His second coming, He does, along with His army (Revelation 19:14). But we see no army in the above Scripture. Rather, we see Jesus remaining in the clouds above the earth and literally snatching us away. The dead in Christ and the living in Christ actually meet Him in the **air**.

And just before that happens, Jesus will give a shout. That word "shout" in Greek is *keleuma* and means "to summon, command, a call." I believe the command will be to, *"come up hither."* Also, the voice of the archangel will be heard. In the ancient Jewish wedding when a bridegroom came for his bride, usually a groomsman would shout, *"behold the bridegroom commeth; go ye out to meet him."* (Matthew 25:6)

So, 1 Thessalonians was written to tell us about the wonderful rapture; what will happen and how it takes place. While 2 Thessalonians was written to reassure the Thessalonians that the rapture had not yet taken place.

In 1 Thessalonians 1:4, Paul praises the church for their steadfastness, endurance, patience and firm faith amid all the persecutions and crushing distresses and afflictions they were experiencing. Things were tough. Because of this, a rumor began circulating that they were in the Tribulation and had missed the rapture.

How does Paul respond? 2 Thessalonians 2:1-3 tells us. *"Now we beseech you, brethren, by the coming of our Lord Jesus Christ, and by our gathering together unto him, That ye be not soon shaken in mind, or be troubled, neither by spirit, nor by word, nor by letter as from us, as that the day of Christ (*the Tribulation*) is at hand. Let no man deceive you by any means: for that day shall not come, except there come a* ***falling away*** *first, and that man of sin be revealed, the son of perdition."*

From this we learn the Tribulation won't come until there is a falling away first and the antichrist is revealed. In Greek, that word for "falling away" is *apostasia* and has these meanings: "a defection from truth, a divorce, a writ of divorcement, to physically remove." So, we have a play on words, indicating that people will leave the Truth (Jesus) and God will divorce them, then physically remove those He has not divorced—in the rapture. **Then** the Tribulation will come.

It's interesting to note that early Bible translators believed *apostasia* referred only to a physical departure rather than a spiritual one. In fact, in the 4th Century, when Jerome translated the New Testament into Latin, he translated *apostasia* as *discessio,* "the departure." Other translators like Wycliffe (1384), Tyndale (1526) and Genova (1608) followed suit by translating it "departing first" all denoting something physical. Then the King James translators changed all that in 1611 by using the phrase "falling away."

But to my mind, the original word, *apostasia,* really says it best because I believe all three meanings will be realized: a spiritual departure, a divorce, then a physical departure.

Now, regarding the antichrist, 2 Thessalonians 2:6-7 tells us this man of sin will be revealed only after the restrainer is taken out of the way. *"For now ye know what withholdeth* (what is restraining) *that he* (the antichrist) *might be revealed in his time. For the mystery of iniquity (*lawlessness*) doth already work: only he who now letteth will let, until he* (the Holy Spirit who restrains) *be taken out of the way."*

Obviously, the Holy Spirit is the restrainer. But we are not told the Holy Spirit will be taken out of the world, only out of the **way**. Even so, the restraining influence of the church must and will be removed. Part of the church's function is to prevail against the gates of hell. During the Tribulation, evil will be unrestrained. It will not be prevailed against.

The Holy Spirit will continue to be active in the world after the rapture. He will not act as restrainer, but He will embolden the 144,000 and the two witnesses, as well as draw people to Jesus. The Bible tells us that multitudes will come to Jesus during the Tribulation. If the Holy Spirit were not on earth, who would draw them to Christ? According to John 16:13, it's the Holy Spirit who leads us into all truth (Jesus and His Word).

But while the Holy Spirit is still working on earth after the rapture, the antichrist will be revealed, and evil will grow worse and worse. It will be a mess but mercifully, we, His bride, will be removed and given our glorified bodies and be joined with Jesus, forever!

We are not appointed unto wrath.

1 Thessalonians 5:9 says, *"For God hath not appointed us to wrath, but to obtain salvation by our Lord Jesus Christ."* Here, that world "salvation" in Greek is *soteria* and means "rescue and safety," as well as "deliver, health, salvation, save, saving." Another play on words. It means we are saved from our sins and rescued from the wrath to come.

Luke 21: 36 tells us to, *"Watch ye therefore, and pray always, that ye may be accounted* ***worthy*** *to* ***escape*** *all* *these things that shall come to pass, and to stand before the Son of man."* Notice the words "worthy" and "escape." That word "worthy" in Greek is *kataxioo* and means "to deem entirely deserving," while that word "escape" in Greek is *ekpheugo* and literally means "to flee out, to run away, escape, to **vanish**." Thus, if we are a genuine born-again believer, a bride without spot or blemish because we are covered by the blood of Jesus and our sins are forgiven, we will flee from, escape, and actually vanish before these things (the Tribulation) come to pass!

Notice, nowhere does it imply we will be protected through it or given power to endure it. The Scripture is clear. **If** we are found worthy, we **will** escape. We will actually **vanish** in the rapture, before the Tribulation begins.

1 Thessalonians 1:10 says we are to, *"wait for his Son from heaven, whom he* (God) *raised from the dead, even Jesus, which* ***delivered*** *us from the wrath to come."* Note that word "delivered" (*rhuomai*). It means "rescued" in Greek. Again, there's no implication here that we will be protected through the Tribulation or in it. Rather, it means we will get out of it. It means we will be rescued from it and won't have to endure it because we're not going to be here.

In Revelation chapters 1-3 Jesus addresses the seven churches. They signified churches that existed in John's day, but they also symbolize various stages in church history as well as various characteristics found in churches throughout the church age. But for this study I will just briefly zero in on two of them: the church of Philadelphia and the church of Laodicea. I believe these are the churches or the characteristics of the church at the end times and are even now apparent.

Laodicea is the lukewarm church that Jesus said He would vomit out. It's the church that *"will not endure sound doctrine"* but will follow their lusts, turning *"from the truth"* to fables and *"doctrines of devils."* (2 Timothy 4:3-4; 1 Timothy 4:1)

But He complimented the church of Philadelphia for keeping His word and not denying His name even though they had, *"little strength."* Because of this, He promised, *"I also will keep thee from the hour of temptation* (the Tribulation) *which shall come upon **all the world**, to try them that dwell upon the earth."* Notice that Jesus said He would keep them from, not through, the hour of testing!

I believe it's the Philadelphia-type church that will be raptured while the Laodicean church, the carnal, apostate church, will remain to face the Tribulation.

The seven-year Tribulation is all about God's wrath. The first half is commonly called the wrath of the Lamb, the second half, the wrath of God.

Further Scriptures include:

- Ephesians 5:6, *"Let no man deceive you with vain words (*false doctrines*) for because of these things cometh the* ***wrath*** *of God upon the children of disobedience."*
- John 3:36, *"He that believeth not on the Son . . . the* ***wrath*** *of God abideth on him."*
- Romans 5:9, *"Much more then, being now justified by his (*Jesus'*) blood, we shall be saved from* ***wrath*** (God's wrath) *through him* (Jesus)*."*
- Romans 1:18, *"For the* ***wrath*** *of God is revealed from heaven against all ungodliness and unrighteousness of men, who hold the truth in unrighteousness."*

If God's wrath is reserved for the unrighteous, the ungodly, the unbelievers, is it reasonable to imagine Jesus would pour out his wrath on His bride? I think not! On the other hand, doesn't God what to raise up a church without spot or blemish? Yes, and this is how Ephesians 5:26-27 tells us He wants to do it. *"That he might sanctify and cleanse it (*the church*) with the washing of water by the word, That he might present it to himself a glorious church, not having spot or wrinkle,* *or any such thing; but that it should be holy and without blemish."*

So, how does Jesus want to prepare His bride? By the washing of water (Jesus is the living water) and by the Word (Jesus is the Word). John 15:3 says, *"Now ye are clean through the word which I have spoken unto you."*

It's clear Jesus doesn't want to cleanse us, his bride, through wrath, by bludgeoning us in the Tribulation, then taking us home, all battered and bruised.

Furthermore, would the rapture be a *"blessed hope"* (Titus 2:13) if we had to experience the wrath of God? If we had to face death at every turn? Or endure the horrendous things that will occur? Would it be a *"comfort"* as described in 1 Thessalonians 4:17-18? Hardly.

One of the biggest arguments believers in the mid-Trib rapture give is that the first half of the Tribulation is the wrath of man and Satan, and not of God. They say that just before God's wrath falls in the second half, then the rapture will occur. But that's not accurate. Jesus is the one who opens the seals, which then open both the trumpet and bowel judgments.

In Revelation 6:16-17, the unsaved people who are alive during the first part of the Tribulation say, *"to the mountains and rocks, Fall on us, and hide us from the face of him that sitteth on the throne, and from the* ***wrath of the Lamb****; For the great day of* ***his*** (Jesus') ***wrath*** *is come; and who shall be able to stand?"*

Revelation 6:16 clearly calls this first half, *"the wrath of the Lamb."* And confirms it again in verse 17 when it says, *"For the great day of his* (Jesus) *wrath is come; and who shall be able to stand?"* This refutes any claim that God in not the author of the first half of the Tribulation. **All** the Tribulation is the wrath of God though He may use Satan and human instruments to bring about some of it.

Mid-Tribers also believe Jesus won't rapture us until the middle of the Tribulation because the first half won't be that bad, and it's only midway through that things really heat up. Yes, the second half of the Tribulation will be worse than the first half, but the first half is terrible, too.

Revelation talks about seven seal, trumpet and bowel judgments occurring during the seven years of trouble. In just the opening of the seals, at the beginning of the Tribulation, great disaster is unleashed through wars, famines, pestilences, the slaughter of believers in Jesus, and massive earthquakes. Half of the world's population will die. A good part of the earth will be destroyed. So that argument doesn't ring true, either.

If you want a picture of just how horrible the beginning of the Tribulation, during the seven seals, will be, I suggest you read Pastor Billy Crone's, *The Seals*. He carefully documents each seal. At the end, you'll wonder how anyone could be left alive!

God has promised to pour our His Spirit on all flesh in the last days. And He's been doing it since the time of the apostles. For almost 2000 years He has been showering us with His grace. God promised that the latter rain will be greater than the former rain. Even now, revival is going on in some countries, especially Muslim ones. Young Muslims are dreaming dreams and seeing visions of Jesus and accepting Him as their Lord and Savior. But what about American? Will American experience one last great revival?

I don't know.

Some are prophesying a great revival is coming to the U.S. But we can't take that for granted. 2 Chronicles 7:14 says, "***If** my people which are called by my name, shall humble themselves, and pray, and seek my face, and turn from their wicked ways; **then** will I* *hear from heaven, and will forgive their sin, and will heal their land."*

Revival will come only if the church repents and prays.

Some Biblical types and shadows of the rapture:

The Bible is to be taken literally. But it's also layered and illustrates types and shadows. Enoch is such a type. He is a picture of the rapture. Hebrews 11:5 tells us Enoch, *"was translated* (changed, removed) *that he should not see death."* Genesis 5:24 says, *"And Enoch walked with God: and he was not: for God took him."* That word "took" in Hebrew is *laqach* and means "to get, fetch, snatch away." It also means "to marry, take a wife"!

Remember that phrase "falling away" in 2 Thessalonians 2:1-3? It said an *apostasia* would take place prior to the Tribulation, and we learned that word meant, "a defection from truth, a divorce, a writing of divorcement, to physically remove." The indication is that people would leave the Truth (Jesus) and Jesus would divorce them, and then physically remove those He has not divorced, meaning His bride, His wife, just like in Genesis 5:24 when God raptured, took, snatched Enoch away because Enoch walked with Him and was considered His wife!

Noah is another type and shadow of the rapture. He was saved out of the flood, not through it. He was removed and put into an ark of safety which God Himself sealed up.

Also, according to Genesis 19:16, Lot was literally removed from Sodom by the angels before its destruction. He was not made to stay in Sodom under God's protection but was removed from the wrath of God which was about to fall on that city.

Moses, at Mt Sinai, (Exodus 19:19-20) is another picture/foreshadowing of the rapture. *"And when the voice of the trumpet sounded long, and waxed louder and louder, Moses spake, and God answered him by a voice. And the Lord came* ***down*** *upon the mount Sinai, and the Lord called Moses* ***up*** *to the top of the mount, and Moses went up."* So, we have a trumpet, God speaking and coming down, and calling Moses to come up. In short, God came down and Moses went up. Just like Jesus will come down in the midst of the clouds and call us up.

Notice how similar Exodus 19:19-20 is to 1 Thessalonians 4:16-17, *"For the Lord himself shall descend from heaven, with a shout, with the voice of the archangel, and with the trump of God: and the dead in Christ shall rise first: Then we which are alive and remain shall be caught up together with them in the clouds, to meet the Lord in the air: and so shall we ever be with the Lord."*

Also, note how similar the Moses scenario is to Revelation 4:1. Jesus just finished giving John the message to the seven churches, and John said, *"After this I looked and behold, a door was opened in heaven: and the first voice which I heard was as it were of a trumpet talking with me; which said, Come up hither and I will shew thee things which must be hereafter."*

Revelation 4:1 is the rapture. Note the open door to heaven and the voice that sounded like a trumpet, and then the command to, "come up hither." After God gives this command, John is immediately in His presence.

John then spends the entire seven years of tribulation in heaven, while the horrific events are played out before him on earth. There is no mention of the church after chapter four. Why? Because the Church Age, the age of grace, is over and focus shifts to Israel.

Other pictures of the rapture and the end times:

The seven feasts of the Lord reveal God's plan and timetable. The first three have already been fulfilled by Jesus: Passover, Unleavened Bread, First Fruits. We are currently in the Feast of Pentecost, which is the church age. Only three feasts remain: Rosh Hashanah or Feast of Trumpets, Yom Kippur or Day of Atonement, and Succoth or Feast of Tabernacles.

Some believe the rapture will occur during Pentecost, signaling the end of the Church Age. According to Jewish tradition, during the Feast of Pentecost there is a celebration called "decorating the bride," and they believe that for a short time there is an open door or portal to heaven. Others believe the rapture will happen during the Feast of Trumpets.

But notice both these feasts come before the Day of Atonement (Yon Kippur) which is a type of the Tribulation, and Succoth or Feast of Tabernacles, which is a type of the millennial kingdom when God/Jesus tabernacles with man.

Then, there are the three major harvests in Israel: barley, wheat, fruit, which add to the picture. Barley (the first harvest) is soft and winnowed without crushing the kernel by throwing it into the air. It's a picture of the believers in Jesus, whose hearts and minds are tender toward God. It's a picture of God harvesting His church through the rapture prior to the Tribulation.

Then comes the wheat harvest. Wheat is a hard grain and needs to be threshed on a threshing floor in order to separate the chaff (shell) from the wheat. In Bible times, it was often threshed by a sled-like board which had rocks embedded in the bottom. The board was harnessed to an ox and dragged over the wheat while a man stood on the board. In Latin, that threshing board is called a *"tribulum."* It's a picture of the harvest of believers during the Tribulation after they are threshed, their hearts softened, and they have come to the Lord.

And finally, we have the fruit harvest, most notably the grape harvest. Grapes are crushed. It speaks of the final harvest where unbelievers are gathered then crush in the winepress of God's wrath. Revelation 14:19 says, *"And the angel thrust in his sickle into the earth, and gathered the vine of the earth, and cast it into the great winepress of the wrath of God."* What an awful picture! The truth is, God doesn't want to crush anyone in His winepress, but He will.

The law of gleaning reveals the true heart of God. In Bible times, owners would leave the four corners of their fields for gleaners—the poor and widows—as a means of providing them food. In Matthew 24:1-31, Jesus is talking about the end times and says in verse 31 that at the end of these days, *"he* (the Son of man) *shall send his angels with a great sound of a trumpet, and they shall gather together his elect from the four* ***winds****, from one end of* ***heaven*** *to the other."* What a beautiful picture of God gleaning the fields after the Tribulation so that not one precious kernel (soul) will be overlooked!

To avoid any confusion, let me drill down a bit. That word "winds" is *anemizo* in Greek and literally means "the four quarters of the earth." And even though the word "heaven" was used instead of "earth," it doesn't imply that angels will be looking for believers outside the earth. Rather, that word "heaven" is *ouranos* and means, "sky, gospel, happiness, Christianity, a mountain, as lifting itself above the plain." I think it's safe to say the angels are gleaning the earth looking for surviving believers in the gospel of Jesus Christ; those who had stayed above or out of the reach of antichrist.

One of my favorite types and shadows is the ancient Jewish wedding, which has many parts and can take a year or longer. First, the bide is purchased. A bride price is agreed upon and paid by the bridegroom; just like Jesus purchased His bride with His blood.

Then the marriage contract is drawn up. It details the obligations and responsibilities of both the bridegroom and bride. The New Testament is our marriage contract. It lays out Jesus' responsibilities to us and ours to Him. He saves us from eternal damnation. He protects us. We hide His word in our heart. We obey His voice, etcetera.

In the Jewish wedding, the bride must accept or reject the offer via a verbal declaration. In like manner, we must accept or reject Jesus' offer of salvation, and voice it. Romans 10:9 says, *"if thou shalt* ***confess with thy mouth*** *the Lord Jesus and shalt believe in thine heart that God hath raised him from the dead, thou shalt be saved."*

Then, once the bride accepts the offer, the groom gives her gifts. Ephesians 1:13-14 tells us that after we believe the salvation message, we are *"sealed with the holy Spirit of promise, which is the earnest of our inheritance."* That word "earnest" in Greek means "pledge given in advance as security for the rest." The Holy Spirit is given to us as a pledge, like an engagement ring. Then the nine gifts of the Spirit are given to us by our bridegroom.

After the giving of the gifts, the bridegroom returns to his father's house to prepare the bridal chamber. In John 14:2-3 Jesus said, *"In my Father's house are many mansions: if it were not so I would have told you. I go to prepare a place for you. And if I go and prepare a place for you, I will come again, and receive you unto myself; that where I am there ye may be also."*

Jesus, the bridegroom, has gone to prepare our bridal chamber, and that chamber is in heaven. Therefore, we must return to heaven in order to complete the wedding. And it's the father who tells his son, the bridegroom, when it's time to bring his bride home. That's why Jesus said in Matthew 24:36, *"But of that day and hour* (the rapture when Jesus comes for His bride) *knowest no man, no, not the angels of heaven, but my Father only."*

Yet all this time, while the bridegroom is away preparing, he and his bride are legally married and can only be separated by a bill of divorcement. Again, we see why that word *apostasia* not only refers to a defection from truth, but a divorce, a writ of divorcement, in additional to being physically removed. Jesus will divorce those who have defected from the truth, and take those who have not, to the bridal chamber to consummate the marriage.

And all this time, the bride must keep herself pure for her bridegroom. But when he returns, it's usually unannounced, sudden and at night. He then takes his bride to the bridal chamber, where the couple will remain for seven days; a perfect picture of the raptured bride hidden away in the heavenly bridal chamber during the seven-year Tribulation.

After being in the bridal chamber for seven days, the bridegroom brings out his bride and joins the guests for a marriage feast. Revelation 19:9 says, *"And he saith unto me. Write, Blessed are they which are called unto the marriage supper of the Lamb."* Then at the end of the Tribulation, Jesus will return to earth with His bride.

And when He does, He will destroy all those gathered against Him. 2 Thessalonians 2:8 says, *"And then shall that Wicked (*Satan*) be revealed, whom the Lord shall consume with the spirit of his mouth, and shall destroy with the brightness of his coming."* Revelation 19:15 says, *"And out of his (*Jesus'*) mouth goeth a sharp sword that with it he should smite the nations . . . and he treadeth the winepress of the fierceness and wrath of Almighty God."* Wow! What a picture, both horrifying and glorious!

Who are the "saints or elect" referred to during the Tribulation?

This refers to the 144,000 and those, both Jew and Gentile, who accept the Lord after the rapture. The words "elect" and "saints" are often used in the Old Testament and refer to the Jews. Isaiah 45:4 calls Israel, *"mine elect."* Isaiah 65:9 also called Jacob and his seed, "mine elect." And Deuteronomy 33:3 says, *"all his saints are in thy hand."* That word "saints" means "sacred, holy." I Samuel 2:9 says, *"He will keep the feet of his saints."* Here, that word means "pious, holy." There are many other examples in the Old Testament, all referring to Jews.

In the New Testament, the word "elect," speaks of believers, as in Colossians 3:12. So does the word, "saints." So, when Matthew 24:22 says, *"except those days should be shortened, there should no flesh be saved: but for the elect's sake those days shall be shortened,"* it refers to both Jews and Gentiles who have accepted Jesus after the rapture and during the Tribulation.

What happens after the rapture?

God transitions from the church to Israel while they fulfil Daniel's 70th Week, also called Jacob's Trouble (the Tribulation). Everything now is centered on Israel and not the church. Romans 11:25b says, *"blindness in part is happened to Israel, until the fullness of the Gentiles be come in."* The rapture indicates that the *"fullness of the Gentiles"* has indeed occurred.

During the Tribulation, this blindness of Israel will be removed. In Roman 11:16-22, God warns against replacing Israel with the church. These Scriptures totally refute "replacement theology." God is not finished with Israel. Rather, Israel becomes the center of attention while God brings them to Himself and prepares them to be the head of nations.

Paul wrote in Acts 17:31 that, *"He* (God) *hath appointed a day, in which he will judge the world in righteousness."* So, after the rapture, judgment begins both on earth and in heaven.

The saints in heaven will appear before the judgment seat of Jesus while the earth reels under God's judgment, His wrath. Revelation 11:18-19 speaks of this. *"And the nations were angry, and thy wrath is come, and the time of the dead, that they should be judged, and that* ***thou shouldest give reward unto thy servants the prophets, and to the saints, and them that fear thy name, small and great****; and shouldest destroy them which destroy the earth. And the temple of God was opened in heaven."*

1 Corinthians 3:13-15 and 2 Corinthians 5:9-10 talk about what's going on in heaven, at the judgment seat of Christ.

That judgment seat is "bema." That word refers to a raised platform. In Roman times. a judge watched racers on the bema to ensure they complied with the rules. Then, when the race was finished, he awarded prizes to the participants; a perfect description of Jesus judging His church.

Hebrews 12:1 says, *"Wherefore seeing we also are compassed about with so great a cloud of witnesses, let us lay aside every weight, and the sin which doth so easily beset us, and let us run with patience the* ***race*** *that is set before us."*

All believers are running a race, and the Bema Judgment will not be a time of condemnation, but a time of rewards. Jesus will hand out crowns according to how we lived our lives for Him.

Some believe there will be a span of time between the rapture and the beginning of the Tribulation, giving Jesus time to hand out the awards at the Bema. Then, after the award ceremony is over, we will enter the bridal chamber for the full seven years of Tribulation.

Aside from the Bema Judgment and the judgment of the earth during the Tribulation, 2 Timothy 4:1 indicates there will be another judgment for nonbelievers. *"I charge thee therefore before God, and the Lord Jesus Christ, who shall judge the quick* (the living) *and the dead at* ***his appearing and his kingdom.****"*

"At his appearing," that's the rapture, and refers to the Bema Judgment. While the second judgment is the White Throne Judgment and occurs at the end of Jesus' 1000-year reign on earth. A very different type of judgment as Revelation 20:11-15 shows. *"And I saw a great* ***white throne****, and him that sat on it, from whose face the earth and the heaven fled away; and there was found no place for them. And I saw the dead, small and great, stand before God; and the books were opened and another book was opened: which is the book of life: and the dead were judged out of those things which were written in the books, according to their works. And the sea gave up the dead which were in it; and death and hell delivered up the dead which were in them: and they were judged every man according to their works. And death and hell were cast into the lake of fire. This is the second death.* ***And whosoever was not found written in the book of life was cast into the lake of fire.****"*

It's sad to think many will imagine their good deeds have balanced out their bad ones when facing God. But good works won't cut it. Ephesians 2:8-9 is clear. *"For by grace are ye saved through faith; and that not of yourselves: it is the gift of God: Not of works, lest any man should boast."* Good deeds won't get anyone listed in the book of life.

There will also be a judgment of the nations, not only for their sins, but for how they treated Israel and for trying to divide their land. (Joel 3:1-21)

So, to wrap it up: while we are in heaven, the Holy Spirit will still be here on earth in order to guide, direct and empower the two witnesses and the 144,000 Jews (12,000 from every tribe except Dan. His place was given to Manasses, Joseph's son. See Revelation 7:6. Some believe this is because antichrist will come from the tribe of Dan. For further insight into this, check our J.R. Church's book, *Daniel Reveals the Blood Line of the Antichrist.* But note, these 144,000 are Jews, NOT the church)

And these 144,000 Jews will evangelize the world and bring people to Jesus so the wheat harvest can be gathered. Millions will come to Christ. But the Holy Spirit will not function in His restraining capacity through the church. The church will be gone. Evil will increase and be unrestrained. There will be a One World Religion headed by the false prophet, and a One World Government headed by antichrist who will overcome the saints. Believers will be slaughtered like cattle. But then, God will punish the kings of the earth (Isaiah 24:19-21), Jesus will return, and Israel will be established as the head of nations.

Two cautionary tales:

The parable of the ten virgins in Matthew 25:1-13 is a warning. Five of the virgins were wise and five were foolish. All ten fell asleep waiting for the bridegroom to come, like so many in the body who are tired of waiting for Jesus' return. Five had extra oil and five ran out. Oil speaks of the Holy Spirit. Not having oil signifies they were not operating under the power of the Holy Spirit, thus were **carnal** Christians. Could these ten virgins represent the two end-time churches? Laodicea and Philadelphia? The carnal, lukewarm, apostate church and the faithful church praised by Jesus? I think so.

In the end, only five went with the bridegroom to the marriage and the *"door was shut,"* so like when God shut the door of Noah's ark. It also reminds me of the "door" that was open in heaven in Revelation 4:1.

When the five foolish virgins shouted, *"Lord Lord, open* (the door) *to us,"* Jesus' answer was, *"I know you not."*

We see something similar in Matthew 24:40-43. Jesus is talking about the end times and says, *"Then shall two be in the field; the one shall be* ***taken****, and the other* ***left****. Two women shall be grinding at the mill; the one shall be* ***taken****, and the other* ***left****."* That word "taken" here in the Greek means, "to take up, to associate oneself in any familiar or intimate act," while "left" means "to forsake, lay aside, leave," which is just what our bridegroom will do at the rapture. He will take His bride and leave the rest.

It is a warning for us to keep our garments clean in readiness for our bridegroom. A horrendous future awaits the world. Knowing what's at stake, believers should earnestly pray for others, so they, too, can escape.

If you don't know the Lord, now is the time to tell Him you are a sinner in need of a Savior and invite Him into your heart. It will change you forever!

www.ingramcontent.com/pod-product-compliance
Lightning Source LLC
Chambersburg PA
CBHW071525040426
42452CB00008B/893
* 9 7 8 0 9 6 5 7 3 8 9 1 0 *